If you are the ceiling to your success, Jennifer Allwood is about to "raise the roof"! You won't feel like you are reading another "rah-rah" girl-power motivational self-help book. Jennifer actually provides a framework to get you unstuck (regardless of your brand of quicksand). With humor and truly relatable stories on every page, I felt like I was having a captivating conversation with my very wise and very funny Jesus-loving BFF. You'll lean in, soak in, and receive messages you know you needed to hear, but more importantly this book will teach you how to get out of your own way.

Chalene Johnson, *New York Times* bestselling author, business and health expert

Jennifer is the kind of spunky self-starter who cheers loud in your corner and offers you the playbook for success! *Fear Is Not the Boss of You* is a guide for best practices; laced with vulnerability and lessons learned, wit and candor, I couldn't put it down. You'll refer back to these pages as you live the courageous life you were made for.

Rebekah Lyons, bestselling author, *Rhythms of Renewal* and *You Are Free*

You will find yourself picking up this book over and over again to hear Jennifer champion you and push you toward your destiny. Using her faith as her compass, Jennifer tells us her journey from a place of openness and honesty that will inspire.

Sarah Jakes Roberts, bestselling author, pastor, and founder of Woman Evolve

Jen doesn't just preach about fear not getting the best of her, she lives it. She is inviting us all in to this message, and I am here to tell that you will not be the same after reading these words.

Jamie Ivey, bestselling author and podcaster

Fear Is Not the Boss of You is the book for the modern-day female who is determined to live a life on purpose. Jennifer gets honest about fear, comparison, and what real courage and confidence look like. If you're feeling stuck, this is the book for you. Get ready to be inspired and motivated, and get the sweetest tough love you'll ever receive to help you take action toward the life of your dreams.

Amy Porterfield, online marketing trainer and
host of *Online Marketing Made Easy* podcast

I highly recommend this book! If you are tired of allowing fear to hold you back from the life you know you were made for, do yourself a favor and grab Jennifer Allwood's book. With the perfect blend of tough love and vulnerable humility, Jen is the encouraging sister you didn't know you needed but always wished you had. Dive into this book, grab an extra copy for a friend, and read expectantly, knowing that God is about to do some big things in your life.

Brian Dixon, cofounder of hope★writers
and author of *Start with Your People*

Jennifer is the real deal, and the transparency and authentic way she leads in her new book *Fear Is Not the Boss of You* will have you rethinking all the systems and strategies out there today. She will lead you face-to-face with your greatest fear, show you how to load up your slingshot and stone, and win the war of your own personal Goliaths. Not only has she done this in her business life, but deep into her personal life she's made it a habit and a lifestyle to dive into the deep end with God on the most important issues.

If fear has plagued you and you feel like you no longer own your own life, this book will be not only a tool but a lifeline. Fear—it's a liar, and it's time for you to stop submitting to its evil ways. You were made for more! Get this book and be sure you get one for a friend too.

Sandi Krakowski, CEO and president of
A Real Change International, Inc.

Jennifer is the life coach, business boss, and truth-telling friend you didn't even know you were looking for. Read this book and be ready to tend to the brilliant fire she'll light in your life.

Myquillyn Smith, *Wall Street Journal* bestselling author of *Cozy Minimalist Home*

I have loved Jennifer Allwood for years, but never did I imagine how her book would undo me. This book is a beautiful and heart-piercing manifesto meant to get us unstuck and living out our God-given callings. I am forever grateful for this woman of God, who goes first by being courageous and unafraid in her message of hope and transformation. Get this book and get yourself unstuck! It's time to offer those gifts to the world, sister.

Edie Wadsworth, author of *All the Pretty Things*

Jennifer Allwood is inspiring and encouraging and won't let you get away with not seeing your true potential. This book is that kind of friend too. Jen holds you to the high standards that she knows you want for yourself but have not had the courage to go for, until now. She never asks you to venture where she herself is not willing to go. She dares to reach beyond her grasp and invites you to reach with her. Jennifer has generously, and with great love and humor, put on these pages what she would say to you over a coffee (or a cocktail). I'm sure you're going to love this book because it's what being friends with Jennifer is really like: truthful and the best.

Suzi Dafnis, CEO of HerBusiness, and finalist of the Ernst & Young Entrepreneur of the Year Award

You are called to so much more, and fear can no longer be your out. Jennifer calls her readers out with a powerful, undeniable testament to the miracle and love of God calling us forward to face our fears and make our dreams come true in every area of life. A must-read for every woman who is ready to become her next and best version of herself.

Kelly Roach, CEO and founder of The Unstoppable Entrepreneur

FEAR IS NOT THE BOSS OF YOU

How to Get Out of Your Head and Live the Life You Were Made For

jennifer allwood

ZONDERVAN
BOOKS

ZONDERVAN BOOKS

Fear Is Not the Boss of You
Copyright © 2020 by Jennifer Allwood

Requests for information should be addressed to:
Zondervan, *3900 Sparks Dr. SE, Grand Rapids, Michigan 49546*

Zondervan titles may be purchased in bulk for educational, business, fundraising, or sales promotional use. For information, please email SpecialMarkets@Zondervan.com.

ISBN 978-0-310-35906-7 (hardcover)

ISBN 978-0-310-35910-4 (international trade paper edition)

ISBN 978-0-310-35908-1 (audio)

ISBN 978-0-310-35907-4 (ebook)

Published in association with Nena Madonia Oshman, Dupree Miller.

Cover photo: Aimee Decker / Radiant Photography
Inside cover photo: Alexandria Dickens / Brighton Road Photography
Interior design: Kait Lamphere

Printed in the United States of America

20 21 22 23 24 25 26 27 /LSC/ 15 14 13 12 11 10 9 8 7 6 5 4 3 2 1

For #AllwoodPartyOf6. Jason, Noah, Easton, Ava, and Ari, you each have my whole heart, and I love you fiercely. You have each sacrificed in this season so I could be obedient to what God asked me to do. I pray our family will continue to do all the big, hard, and scary things God asks each of us to do with grateful, obedient hearts. I am the biggest fan of each of you.

And for every woman who has a little tug in her heart that makes her wonder if there is more to life than where she currently is. Yes, friend, there is. Chase Jesus and you're sure to find it.

THE Lord *announces* THE WORD,

AND THE *women* WHO PROCLAIM IT ARE A MIGHTY *Throng.*

PSALM 68:11

CONTENTS

one

ARE YOU A GIRL WHO IS . . .

two

HOW DID YOU GET HERE?

three

ARE YOU READY FOR CHANGE?

four
WHAT'S A GIRL TO DO?

five
WHAT HAPPENS NEXT?

part
ONE

ARE YOU A GIRL
WHO IS . . .

Familiar
FEELS GOOD
EVEN WHEN
IT IS *bad.*

chapter one

STUCK?

Growth is painful. Change is painful.
But nothing is as painful as staying
stuck somewhere you don't belong.
—MANDY HALE

Being stuck stinks.

And the reason being stuck stinks is that it sucks the life out of you. It makes you feel hopeless about your current situation. It makes you feel lesser than because you should be able to get yourself out of the rut you're in. It gets you into all sorts of comparison traps and has a way of convincing you that things will alllllllllways be this way.

And I hate that about "stuck." Because "stuck" whispers generalizations and lies like "always" and "you can never" and "if only." And even though it's a whisper, over time you get so used to the sound of stuck in your own head that it doesn't require shouting anymore.

You have resigned yourself to thinking that your situation or your life or your relationship or your business will always be the way it is now, and you just need to accept that.

And as if that isn't bad enough, "stuck" sucks the life out of others. You weren't meant to stay stuck, and so inevitably you won't be the best wife/mother/daughter/sister/friend you can be for someone else when you're knee-deep in it. Your kids will suffer. Your spouse will suffer. And the world suffers because it's so in need of what you have. But in your "stuck-ness," you can't give all you have, because you are not free.

When you're stuck, you stay small. And when you stay small, you can't influence others. And when others go un-influenced, they will stay stuck too. It's a cat-chasing-its-tail situation.

This is why you can't stay stuck.

And girl, I've got good news for you. You don't have to stay stuck and overwhelmed forever. You *are* able to do hard things and do them while you are still afraid. But you have to get unstuck first.

Sometimes being stuck is a result of our bad decisions, and sometimes not.

Sometimes being stuck happens *to* us and sometimes it happens *because* of us. Do I need to say that a little louder for the girls in the back?

And trust me when I say, I have been stuck many times, in many ways, and in many, *many* different seasons.

In my twenties I was stuck in a bad relationship. I was in a new city where I didn't know many people, with a mortgage to pay and no extra money. I told myself that I didn't have many options other than staying together with this guy. If I broke it off, I would be alone, lonely, broke, and struggling. None of which sounded very appealing.

So even though the relationship was not good or healthy, the only option I felt I had was convincing myself that "it wasn't really that bad." (Have you ever told yourself that?) Feeling option-less kept me stuck in a relationship for way too long for all the wrong reasons.

Stuck can be dangerous.

I can remember feeling so stinkin' stuck when the kids were little. Jason and I had decided that I would stay home with the children while he worked a sales job outside the home, and even though I was nuts about the kiddos and ridiculously grateful that we were able to work out financially how I could be home, I still felt stuck. (Related: you can be doing the right thing and still feel stuck.)

I was stuck watching *Bob the Builder* for the hundredth time in a row. I was stuck changing diapers. I was stuck running kids back and forth to mom's day out.

I knew it was for a season and I shouldn't wish it away, but I lost a lot of myself during those days of raising babies and feeling stuck. And then I felt guilty about my feelings because so many women would have traded spots with me in a heartbeat. So then I was stuck *and* trying to convince myself I shouldn't feel that way, which eventually led to bitterness. And bitterness steals your joy.

Stuck steals from you, my friend.

Jason and I have gone through more than one season in our marriage where our finances were in the gutter and we were stuck. Stuck barely making the bills. Stuck trying to figure out how to get out of debt. Stuck at home not being able to take vacations. Stuck in the same house because we couldn't afford another. Stuck shopping at garage sales and thrift stores. Stuck in jobs we didn't love or even enjoy, but we had to do what we had to do 'cuz we had backed ourselves into a corner and we were stuck.

Stuck robs you of options.

For years I was stuck in a desk job that I hated. Oh, it looked so good on the outside with my pager and my pantyhose (those were the good ol' days), but I was dying a slow death stuck in that cubicle, day in and day out. For years I remember thinking, isn't there more to life than this? (Spoiler alert if you are stuck too: yes, there is.)

Stuck keeps you way too long in places you aren't supposed to be.

Maybe you can relate to some of this. Maybe you have sensed there is more to life than what you are currently experiencing, but you don't know how to get there and you don't know where *there* even is. Or the fear of failing, fear of something new, or fear of judgment keeps you stuck.

Maybe you want to start something new, do something different, try something you never have before, but you can't get unstuck enough even to take the first step. Every time you make an effort to take a step in the direction you want to go, the wind gets knocked out of your sails. I get it, girl. I've been there.

Maybe you know in your soul you have settled for the wrong man, the wrong job, the wrong city, or doing the wrong thing. I have done all that and then some.

Or maybe you've just become complacent. You've allowed yourself to get stuck in a rut of just going through the motions. You go to work. You come home. You do the dishes. You watch the TV. Then you pass out in bed. And rinse and repeat day after day until you retire and die.

It's no wonder you feel like you are slowly dying on the inside. Your soul is craving more! You were never meant for that.

Because complacency is a form of stuck.

And stuck kills.

It kills dreams. And confidence. And relationships. And progress. Stuck kills businesses and opportunities and will always keep you smaller than you are meant to be.

We live in a world where we have more options than ever before. People can communicate and work from anywhere in the world because of cell phones and technology. I can go online right now and have toilet paper delivered to my house in two hours. I can travel around any city in the world in an Uber without ever having to rent a car or drive myself. I can hire someone to do my personal grocery shopping and bring it into my kitchen the same afternoon.

We have information at our fingertips 24/7 and options like we've never had before. What a wonderful time to be alive, right?

But even with more options than ever before, we are also stuck with fear more than ever before.

Years ago, I became fascinated with the online space. I loved social media and found that it allowed me to let my freak flag fly a little bit while also allowing me the ability to delete comments and edit my thoughts, which to an introvert feels super safe.

At the time, I was running a decorative painting business that was local to my Kansas City area only. But I was tired of managing people locally and recognized if I got into this internet thing, I could teach people nationwide how to paint. I hired a business coach to help me pivot into running my business online and show me how to get from point A to point B as quickly as possible.

One afternoon, I was on a call with my business coach Sandi Krakowski. Sandi was what my kids call "Facebook Famous," so I expected to discuss a new Facebook ad strategy with her, or how I should set up some sexy marketing funnel. But instead she told me that she had been praying about our coaching call and felt like she was supposed to ask me a question.

"What is it that you want?" she asked.

What the what? I froze.

What was it that I wanted? No one had ever asked me that before. Sure, I had been asked what I wanted for dinner and what I wanted for Christmas, but this was a much deeper, bigger question. This was a "What do you want from life?" kind of question. And I, embarrassingly enough, had no idea.

I was fortyish when this happened. I know it sounds morbid, but for all practical purposes, I knew I was roughly halfway to my life being over. How could I *not know* what I wanted from life?

The truth was . . . no one had ever asked me.

And the other more important truth was . . . I had never asked myself.

The question "What is it that you want?" sounded to me like a "What kind of life are you dreaming of?" type of question. And up to that point, I, perhaps like you, had spent my entire life in many stages/modes that didn't include room for dreaming.

WHAT IS IT THAT YOU *want?*

Up to that point, I had been in get-a-degree mode. Get-married mode. Get-a-good-job mode. In survival mode. In baby-rearing mode. In making-the-mortgage mode. What I "wanted" didn't really register much. I had simply been on autopilot.

See, most of my life I had been what I like to call an SRP. A "Super Responsible Person." Probably half of you reading this are SRPs and the other half of you are married to them, so you will totally understand.

SRPs do not go through life wondering, "What is it that I want?" Super responsible people go through life doing the logical, responsible things that need to be done and doing what others expect of them.

We pay the mortgage early. We stay in jobs with 401(k) matches. We have ample life insurance. We Dave Ramsey our way through debt. We work two jobs if needed. *We.take.care.of.stuff.* But we don't sit around wondering what we want.

Most of the time, we super responsible people aren't dreamers. We are doers.

We do what we need to because it doesn't even occur to us not to. Can you relate?

And one of the things that bothered me about that question from Sandi is that I had no idea what I wanted out of my business or my life. I was stuck just living day to day without even considering, *What is this all even for?*

I had never really considered what I wanted.

I know at one time I wanted all the kids potty trained. I wanted a new SUV. I wanted my waist back. But she was asking me to dig deeper, and it was realllllly uncomfortable.

Just recently I discovered that even Jesus asked people what they wanted. "What do you want me to do for you?" (Matthew 20:32).

Whoa. I tried to imagine what would happen if it wasn't Sandi who asked me what I wanted, but Jesus. How lame would that be if I couldn't even come up with an answer for Jesus? Not good, Jen, not good.

Since that coaching call, I have tried to really determine what it is that I'm hoping to get out of this ONE lifetime.

Because we gotta know where we want to go, sis. Or better yet, where God wants us to go.

So often, part of my being stuck was about my circumstances and my fear—which we'll talk about later—but a lot of it was also my lack of vision. I had no idea where I wanted to go or what I wanted to do. And it's hard to leave a place you are stuck in emotionally or physically or spiritually if you have no idea where you are going *to*.

We stay stuck because at least we know stuck. And at least stuck is familiar. And unfortunately, familiar feels good even when it is bad.

So many socially, morally, and spiritually conscious people are stuck simply because they have been trained to do what is expected of them and not what they want or what God nudges them to do. Oh, if you're an SRP, you're going to get free from that in this book, my friend. Some of your stuckness is not your fault.

Since starting my online business, there are so many times when I'm about to launch something new and I just feel stuck or scared. I struggle to get out of my own way. I worry about what people will think, and it causes me to delay doing what I know I'm supposed to. Stuck, for me, often feels like standing on the internet naked, and who on earth wants to do that, right?

So I want you to know I have been where you are. I have felt the same nagging suspicion that I should be doing something bigger, different, more meaningful, all the things.

I have had your exact "I can't put my finger on what it is, but I know I want more" feeling. I have been paralyzed with fear and settled for less than God's best for me for more reasons than I can list here.

And what has happened to me, and what I see happening so often to other people, is that they get really stinkin' comfortable in their stuck. And they eventually take up camp in Stuck-ville, surrounded by other stuck people. And they live there so long and see people just like them so much that they often don't even recognize they are stuck anymore.

But it doesn't have to be like that. I want you to know there is so much hope. If you are stuck, scared, or overwhelmed and trapped in your own head, you are like so many of the women I work with. If you are wanting to do something that feels meaningful and significant to you, you're in the right place. You are like so many of the women I coach. You are gifted in so many ways but dangling somewhere in between "I think I can" and "Who do I even think I am?"

And yes, girl, in case you aren't entirely sure, there *is* more for you. God *does* have more for you than this.

And I'm gonna show you how to get it.

In the rest of this book, I am going to show you how to go from being stuck and scared to being free. I'm going to show you how you can have a different life than the one you have today, without feeling guilty or fearful or overwhelmed. I'm going to tell you how to show up for your own life.

Friend, the God of the universe is on your side and in your corner and partnering with you for a life that is wild and free and anything but average. Average people are stuck. They let their fear control their actions. They let their feelings become their boss. But you are not that person. Fear is not the boss of you. You are completely capable of having a life filled with peace and deep joy and expectancy.

A life without being stuck. A life without all the overwhelmed. And a life where you have learned how to do things afraid so much that it just becomes natural to you.

This is a life worth living.

Are you ready?

chapter two

OVERWHELMED?

*Right or wrong, make a decision. The
world is paved with flat squirrels who
couldn't make up their mind.*
—ANONYMOUS

I hate the saying "God will never give you more than you can handle." Oh really?

Tell that to the new widow with four kids. Tell that to the family fighting cancer . . . again. Tell that to the overworked, underpaid, barely-hanging-on-by-her-fingernails single mom.

We are often given more than we can handle, but we are never given more than *God* can handle. Can I get an amen?

Life is just so stinkin' busy, and it seems like there really isn't a break from it. One of the greatest lies that Jason and I tell each other is that "after this season, it will really slow down." Ha!

These days, "overwhelmed" isn't just something that affects a few people. "Overwhelmed" is rampant. It's widespread. It's the new normal.

Maybe you didn't identify with "stuck" in the last chapter, but more than likely you can identify with "overwhelmed." I mean, do you even know anyone "underwhelmed"? If so, I want to meet this unicorn.

I think this is why I lose my mind when I hear my kids say they are bored. Let me hand you my to-do list, sweet daughter. I'll see your boredom and raise you my overwhelmed.

Being overwhelmed for a season is manageable and probably even normal. It's overwhelming to bring home a new baby. It's overwhelming to take care of the kids when your husband is out of town. It's overwhelming to prepare to move and launch a kiddo to college at the same time. But what isn't normal is consistently being overwhelmed day in and day out. Month after month and year after year. And what's not okay is to let yourself get trapped in your own head, where being overwhelmed stops you from making decisions.

Overwhelmed happens when there are sooooooo many options to choose from and you have no idea which one to choose, or you've been making so many decisions that you just can't handle one more. Your mind starts going in circles, trapping you in all the options, and you end up choosing nothing.

A classic example of this is the worst question any husband can ask an overwhelmed wife: "Where do you want to eat?" Ohmygooooooodness, that question has caused more arguments for Jason and me. Anyone else?

My standard answer is, "You decide, and I'll let you know if I don't like where you pick." Inevitably, I don't like his idea. I don't want to make the decision, but I do want full permission to have veto power. And all the wives said, "Amen."

Overwhelmed happens too when you begin to overthink things. You get stuck in your own head and begin to second-guess yourself. You make no decisions or poor decisions based on your current feelings of being overwhelmed, and it robs you of clarity and joy.

Truth: you are reading the fourth version of this book. Just typing that makes me want to cuss. I know my editor wanted to kill me, but I convinced her that God had a special place in heaven for her for putting up with me and that she would forfeit that special spot if she killed me. And here I still am.

But I got 20,000 words in on this book and suddenly overthought it to death and decided it was garbage. So I started a second time and picked that apart also. Somewhere in the middle of the third version, I decided my writing was crap, I was crap, everything was crap, and I started again. #facepalm. It took me over 150,000 words to write a 65,000-word book. That is overthinking things if I have ever seen it. And my writing confidence was really in the gutter.

You see, being stuck and overwhelmed will always drag us down and convince us there is something wrong with us. I've been blogging for twelve years. I have been writing social media posts for ten years. I know I can write. But the overwhelmingness of writing an entire *book* was apparently more than my chaotic, blonde-headed brain could digest. For the past few months of writing this book, I have been a poster child for being overwhelmed and overthinking. There's nothing quite like going through, in real time, what you are writing about. The irony of that is not lost on me.

The problem with overthinking things and getting stuck in your own head is it perpetuates staying stuck. Overwhelmed people will often be so scared of making the wrong decision that they will make *no* decision. And, oh friend. No decision definitely *is* a decision. When your spouse asked you to marry him, if you had *not* given him an answer, your decision was obviously a no . . . which he would have known by default since you didn't give him a yes.

This is the problem with being overwhelmed. Often when you can't think clearly enough to make a decision, by default it becomes a no.

There is a meme that you can find all over Pinterest and in

any self-help book that says, "Fear kills more dreams than failure ever will." But I have a different take.

I think *inaction* kills more dreams than anything else does. This is why it is so important that you get over being overwhelmed. And get unstuck enough to do something. *It's so you can get to work doing what you are supposed to be doing.*

I've noticed something else about myself recently. When I am overwhelmed, I avoid or self-protect by doing other things.

Example: The other day I needed to hit a deadline for this book, and I somehow found myself cleaning out

Inaction kills MORE DREAMS THAN ANYTHING ELSE DOES.

my closet. Me . . . the woman who keeps everything and hates to purge and therefore never cleans out her closet was cleaning out her closet. Even though I had a *big* deadline that day, I was doing a *little* task.

This is a classic situation of getting overwhelmed, and then doing dumb stuff—unimportant tasks that were totally unrelated things that have nothing to do with the bigger thing I needed to be doing.

Sound familiar?

When we are overwhelmed, we immediately begin to self-protect.

When we self-protect, we shield ourselves from the discomfort of doing a hard thing by conquering an easy thing (throwing out old jeans) instead. We feel like we accomplished something without putting ourselves at too much risk.

Did you hear that?

We will do something that we know we can master because an overwhelmed woman still wants a trophy of some kind. She wants a win on something. Something smaller, something safer.

This is why when you need to do something hard, you may find yourself on Instagram to see who commented on your post (there's a chemical reaction in your brain that signals *win* when you receive online affirmation). Or you do something like sort through the mail when you should be filling out that application for college (but at least the bills are paid).

WHEN FACED WITH A *hard thing,* WE OFTEN CHOOSE AN *easy win* INSTEAD.

See, we all want to feel like a rock star at something . . . anything, don't we? And that is why we get on the crazy train and do things like sort our summer shorts into long, medium, and probably-can't-ever-wear-again lengths when we need to be writing a book. #truestory.

Then, all too often, we shame ourselves for protecting ourselves. Because in our minds, we feel like working on those big, hard, and scary things could kill us.

Now, logically you know that deciding who to hire for a job or where to go to med school or how to start your first Etsy account won't kill you. But your brain is still signaling that these are scary territories, things you've not done before, so proceed with caution. And you self-protect to self-preserve.

You are supposed to do that. Being stuck and overwhelmed isn't all your fault. But it *is* a vicious cycle that traps you in your own head, and you gotta get out.

Honestly, we weren't meant to have so many choices. Back in the day, your choices were to go out and kill a bear for dinner, or to go out and kill a wild boar. There was no smorgasbord of choices assaulting our minds and our eyes every single day.

I saw this all the time in the decorative painting business that I owned for seventeen years. I loved learning new painting techniques and doing sample boards. I couldn't wait to get the samples into my portfolio so that I could dazzle all my potential clients with the possibilities for their home.

But what I noticed is that if I took my entire portfolio in with me, with every one of my paint samples, my clients would have a hard time deciding. It would frustrate me because it would make me feel like they didn't like my work, when in reality, because there was so much to choose from, *they couldn't choose at all.*

Eventually I got smart and figured out that less was more. If I knew someone was looking for light-textured walls, I would take in only three or four different texture samples to show them. With fewer options, they felt less overwhelmed and could make decisions much more quickly. It saved us all time and headaches.

That was such an eye opener for me.

Being overwhelmed can easily put us in the pit. In the pit of comparison (we wonder why she is able to handle the pressure and I am not). In the pit of jealousy (because I want to handle things like she does). And the pit of stuck (since I don't know how to do it like that, I won't do it at all).

That pit ain't for you, sis. God has a better place picked out for you than that. A place that has fur pillows, shag rugs, and glittery accessories. Not the stench of the place you've been in . . . overwhelmed and stuck.

And I want to help you figure out how to get to that place of freedom, but before that, we need to talk about why you have become stuck and overwhelmed in the first place.

Because sometimes knowing how you ended up in a place is the ticket to getting out!

Buckle up, because it's time to talk about fear.

chapter three

SCARED?

It's like the smarter you are,
the more things can scare you.
—KATHERINE PATERSON,
BRIDGE TO TERABITHIA

So if you're currently feeling overwhelmed and stuck, I would bet my last Hobby Lobby 40-percent-off coupon that you're also all tied up in knots of fear.

You fear you're gonna be stuck forever.

If you try something to get unstuck, you fear you will fail miserably and everyone will see it. Or you fear that the new thing will be worse than being stuck.

Or perhaps you're overwhelmed with all your choices, and the fear of making the wrong one makes you freeze.

Any of this sound familiar?

You fear saying no to people, so you say yes to that PTA position or church volunteer job you have no time for. Which just makes you more overwhelmed. As does your fear of doing the wrong thing, or doing the right thing in the wrong way or at the wrong time.

Basically, being stuck, being scared, and being overwhelmed are all sister wives, and it isn't a good relationship. They all come back to the fear of something. They all take up camp in the same place and basically look the same and smell the same, and they all lead you down the same road of confusion and destruction.

Fear makes us behave in ways that shock ourselves, because logically we know the fear makes no sense.

We don't apply for a job promotion that we know we are totally qualified for because we're afraid of not being ready or not getting it. Or worse, we fear that we WILL get it and then need to actually do the thing we said we can do.

Fear will make you hold back from announcing a recent business success because you're afraid of being judged by family members you really don't like that much anyway.

Fear will make you delay hitting publish on that website you spent months building and thousands of dollars creating.

Fear will make you stay in a place you have outgrown for longer than you should stay, because what if it's worse "over there"?

I learned this the hard way.

At age twenty-five, I was dating Jason and working full-time at an insurance company. I didn't love the job, but as an SRP, I was terrified to do anything different than stay a slave to the cubicle.

Not only did I stay, but I even went back to college to finish my degree in order to get a better job in a company I didn't love and in an industry that I hated. OMGosh, even typing that now, I want to smack myself.

I'd gone to college for one year right out of high school, but I blew my academic scholarship because my grades reflected my poor choices ("poor choices" is code for boys and beer). The truth is, at twenty-five I probably wanted to go back to school to prove I could finish more than I actually wanted a degree. So I started taking night classes, not entirely sure what for.

After a couple of years, I was done with my prerequisites, and it was time to declare a major. I'll never forget the day I sat in my adviser's office, and she asked what degree I was interested in.

I told her how I loved houses. I'd purchased my first home at the age of twenty-one, because as a super responsible person I didn't like the idea of wasting money on rent. (What a huge responsibility for a twenty-one-year-old. My friends were in the bar buying quarter margaritas, and I was working overtime to pay mortgage insurance.)

But I decorated that little house pretty darned cute, if I don't mind saying so myself. I was a professional at garage-sale finds and thrift-store treasures and repainting and repurposing. Creating a space that I loved and felt good in brought me deep joy, and I found I was a natural at it. I could somehow see how to put a room together and make colors work, and it was *the thing* that tripped my trigger.

My mom had always decorated our home beautifully. My favorite aunt, Barb, sold home decor through Home Interiors and Gifts, and my grandmother loved all things fancy. I came from a long line of decorating women and was passionate about it. I crackled walls before crackle was a thing, and I was designing my small master bedroom closet on a piece of paper for a contractor to build before California Closets was even on the internet.

You gotta understand, this was back in the early 1990s, when Google was barely here. Pinterest was not even a twinkle in the internet's eye, and HGTV was officially on the air, but Hilde was busy stapling flowers to bathrooms and gluing hay on people's walls. For the love.

So the idea of becoming a professional decorator who actually made real money wasn't a thing I'd seen done. I didn't know any decorators or know anyone who used a decorator. I assumed people weren't banging down the door to get hay glued to their walls (I mean, did you see that episode? I am still scarred by it).

I told the adviser that too. And then I made the critical mistake that day of looking at my potential career options through the eyes of my own checkbook. I hope someone just read that right. Too often we base our decisions off our current circumstances (how much money we have or how much we currently know or who we currently are) instead of on the potential down the road.

I knew I couldn't afford a decorator. Therefore, I didn't think *other* people could either. What a knucklehead I was! That was terrible logic! But when I knew better, I did better. And you'll know better in a minute too. Xoxo.

I told the adviser that I was thinking of a degree in computers, because I knew computers were becoming "a thing." That makes me sound about a hundred years old, doesn't it? I knew nothing about computers. Nothing. I knew they had a keyboard, and I knew that in Mr. Yackey's typing class, I was able to type fifty-five words per minute, thank you very much. But someone told me computer jobs were paying well, and I loved the idea of making a lot of money. So I settled on the computer degree because I feared I couldn't make money with decorating.

Now before you start sending me hate mail, can we just be honest that pretty much everybody wishes they made more money? Money in and of itself is not a bad thing. As Grant Cardone said, "Money can't buy happiness, but poverty can't buy anything." Can I get an amen?

I knew I had potential to make great money from computers, and that felt like a safer bet to me than decorating, which made me scared that I would starve to death. So out of fear, I chose "safe."

We all like safe. It's human nature to avoid hard things, and our normal tendency is to drift toward the safe thing in order to protect ourselves. I mean, who honestly likes to be scared?

Women especially like "safe."

Women who have gone through hard things will almost always

choose safe, because for the love of all things holy, they don't want to go back to going through hard things again.

A woman who feels stuck, overwhelmed, and scared will almost always choose safe, because choosing anything else makes her feel very vulnerable, and she will avoid vulnerable at all costs. She's already got enough big feelings as someone who's scared, stuck, and overwhelmed.

WOMEN WHO HAVE GONE THROUGH *hard things* WILL ALMOST ALWAYS *choose safe.*

So because of my fear, I decided right then and there that I would get a degree in computers so that I would have the potential for a great income one day.

I knew in my heart of hearts that I was making the wrong decision that day. I remember having a nagging feeling that a computer degree was an awful fit for me. It was a lump-in-the-pit-of-my-belly feeling that I ignored as I picked classes for my fall schedule.

In retrospect, that feeling was God trying to convince me to do the bigger, harder, scarier thing I felt called to, because as the creator of the universe, He had put that love of pretty things in me for a specific reason. But although I had become a Christian at age sixteen, I'd fallen off the faith wagon during my crazy year in college. It wasn't until many years later that I really came back, so making a big life decision about my degree didn't include prayer or godly counsel. It included a pack of Marlboro Light 100's to calm my nerves and doing what seemed least scary in that moment . . . computers.

I picked a degree and a future I had no interest in out of fear of messing up the safety and security of the life I'd built.

Can you relate? Gosh, I hate fear so much. It's such a con artist and such a thief.

It took me five long years of working full-time during the day and going to school nights and weekends to get my degree in Computer Based Information Systems (what does that even mean?).

I was thirty years old and married by the time graduation rolled around, and I was feeling like a rock star because the end of night school was in sight.

One weekend, not long before graduation, Jason and I went to a home show in Kansas City because I was still obsessed with houses. As a newly married couple, Jason and I had purchased a new home, and I was itching to decorate it. And there at the show, tucked in one of the aisles between the shutters and the air conditioners and the deck remodelers, was a talented couple who taught classes on decorative and faux painting. Until that moment, I didn't even know what that was.

As soon as I walked into their booth, I felt my heart begin to race. You creatives get this. It was like being surrounded with colorful, delicious eye candy. Everywhere I looked there was more stimulating goodness—all these amazing textures and colors that could be put onto walls and cabinets. My mind was racing with the possibilities for our own home.

This couple taught weekend-long painting classes, and I signed up to go to one, just for fun. (Side note: this is what I call a *gateway drug*. God often uses something you aren't even looking for to pivot you and lead you to your calling. It often seems like something little and exciting, but it's often setting you up for the big thing God really wants you to do.)

My friend, that weekend changed my life . . . and my career and my future. I became obsessed with paint. With the smell, the feel, the colors, the textures, and how I could use it to make anything pretty!

Even though I was less than a month out from graduating with honors with my computer degree, I went home and told my husband I wanted to start a painting company as a side hustle to my day job. Thank God that he gave me the thumbs-up on my idea, because it made no sense.

I graduated and began working in my blah, blah, blah job of software development. Insert all the yawning gifs. I am so grateful for smart people who understand computers, but I was not and am not one of them.

I wore my pantyhose and fancy pager (are you old enough to remember those?), and I should have felt like hot stuff, but I was dying on the inside. I could never shake the idea that there had to be more to life than this. I couldn't stand watching the clock until 5:00 every day, the commute, the meetings, the schedule. Ew. I'm still triggered just thinking about it.

It was *not* who I was, but I was so scared to do anything else that I stayed stuck in a job that wasn't for me, and then hated myself for not having the guts to do something that I wanted to do. I knew I'd never quit the computer gig to do painting full-time, though, because SRPs don't give up their 401(k) matches to roll the dice on being self-employed. They just don't.

Enter divine intervention. (That's code for God is big enough to sort out the mess I made and still get me to do what I was supposed to be doing. That's why He's God.)

I started The Magic Brush (I know, cheesy) in 2000 and painted on nights and weekends after working at the computer job all day. I wasted my employer's time Monday through Friday searching the internet for new painting ideas and dreaming about having a job that I didn't hate every day. Insert all the hanging head emojis, because Jen, what were you doin', girl?

Eventually, though, my day job caught on to the fact that I was wasting their time and they laid me off. Thank the Lord, because otherwise I would have grown old and died there in that cubicle with pantyhose on.

Now that I was jobless, though, I decided to try to make something out of this little painting gig. If I could get enough customers, maybe I wouldn't have to go back to that pantyhose and pager life.

And guess what? It worked. I looked up every designer and decorator in my part of Kansas City in the Yellow Pages (a dinosaur of a book) and either called or showed up to every one of them.

Now, as an introvert, I am happy to never leave home and talk to no one. But desperation will make a girl do things she otherwise wouldn't. God can work with desperate! I was willing to do anything to avoid going back to corporate America.

I landed some amazing painting jobs with some high-end decorators and homes, and I ended up owning that painting company for seventeen years and working in three homes for *Extreme Makeover: Home Edition.* Our painting was in sought-after homes in parades, on TV, and in magazines. And that eventually led me to coaching other creative women on how to build their local businesses online. It was my honor to own that company for so long.

Yes, my life is lovely without having that decorating degree, but I'll always know that fear made me choose safe, and it cost me years (five, to be exact) of life while I slugged it out in night school. And that makes me sad.

Sad enough, in fact, to write a book for you so that I can help you to do things differently. I am writing for you the book I needed at that time in my life.

We know that fear is a liar. But it's a reallllllllly good one, isn't it?

Fear will convince you to wait, 'cuz surely if you're scared, it must be bad timing.

Fear will convince you to settle for less than what you deserve. I love the saying by Bob Goff, "Fear and insecurity will always try to talk us into settling for lesser things." Isn't that the truth?

We can all think of someone who is in a horrible relationship. And to us it's so obvious, right? Why did she settle for that knucklehead? But I guarantee you, she settled out of fear. Fear that no one better would come along. Fear that she would be alone forever.

> FEAR WILL CONVINCE YOU TO SETTLE FOR LESS THAN *God's best.*

Fear makes us hide. It makes us play small so that others won't see us. Sometimes that means *really* small.

Anyone else got an issue with feeling exposed?

I'm married to a complete extrovert. Jason is the life of the party, 100 percent fine with getting all the attention, all the time. He's the one at wedding receptions pulling a necktie back and forth between his legs on the dance floor. There may or may not be proof of this on our wedding video.

In other words, Jason doesn't mind being seen. In fact, he enjoys eyeballs on him. I, on the other hand, do not. Let.me.hide.

When we go to school basketball games together and we get there after the game starts, I will go under the dark, smelly bleachers rather than cross the floor in front of everyone. If we're at a football game, I'll sit in the first open seat I see, even if it's low and the view is bad, in order to get out of everyone's view and blend in.

I have always been this way. My fear of being seen isn't a new thing since being successful in my business, but the success has amplified it and makes me want to hide even more.

Maybe you don't have a fear of failure or a fear of being seen. But do you have a fear of success? A fear that if you become successful you won't be able to keep up, to sustain it, to keep it?

I coach over three thousand businesswomen every month in my paid coaching groups, and I can tell you with as much absolute certainty as me sitting here eating a bag of potato chips in bed right now that there are as many women scared to *succeed* as there are scared to *fail*. Oh, yes. That's the truth right there.

We are soooo much more comfortable in struggle than we are in success. The struggle bus is comfortable, isn't it? It's got plenty of seating, an air conditioner to keep us cool, and we can depend on it to show up.

Often, when we've been stuck and struggling for so long, it becomes the place we know best and where we're the most comfortable.

Years ago, I did a course on how to paint furniture. It was a $47 class that would last a few hours, and I prayed for 200 signups. Well, I hit 100 signups and was like *yes, girl*. Then I hit 200 people (which I prayed for), and I did a happy dance. Then I hit 300 signups, and panic started to set in a little bit. What in tarnation was happening? And then I hit 400 signups and I pitched a fit on the inside. You would think I would have been rejoicing at doubling my goal and doubling what I asked God for. But suddenly I felt very unworthy, and fear kicked in like the flu bug at elementary school. I was in the fetal position sucking my thumb quicker than you can say Tamiflu. I couldn't come to terms with *that many* people signing up. Now I had to deliver. And what if they all saw through me?

My best business buddy is Carrie Robiana, an incredibly powerful businesswoman and podcaster. She started running Facebook ads a few years ago to grow her following on social media, and they were working super well. When she hit 20,000 followers, I called to congratulate her. And I can remember my shock when she told me that she'd turned the ad off. Why? It was working so well. She said she did it impulsively because the success of it scared her. Carrie worried that she wouldn't be able to handle her growing business. And in a panic, she turned off success.

I'm telling you, people (me included) do weird things all the time when we start to see a little success.

But fear isn't just about business. There are studies that show sometimes women will *not* lose weight that they need to for fear of drawing unwanted attention to themselves or fear of being noticed.

Fear does strange things to us. It makes us act irrationally and behave in ways we know are not good for us.

So between being stuck, overwhelmed, and scared, it's no wonder so many women are playing small. It feels like so much work is required to get past those things, doesn't it?

Friend, I want you to know that your feelings are not always your fault. There are some things going on in the world and in life that are partly responsible for you being where you are today.

In the next chapter, we will figure out who to blame for your big feelings of being stuck, overwhelmed, and scared, so we can start to change them. Sound fun?

Who to blame it all on is coming up next!

part

TWO

HOW DID YOU
GET HERE?

I KNEW I NEEDED A *break* BECAUSE

I NEEDED A

breakthrough.

chapter four

WATCHING OTHER PEOPLE WIN

*The fastest way to kill something special
is to compare it to something else.*
—CRAIG GROESCHEL

There are so many things conspiring against you, sis, and these things are legit challenging. Yes, at the end of the day, we are all grown-ups and it's our job and our responsibility to deal with these things. But I want you to know right up front that part of why you feel stuck and scared is not your fault.

Let's start with social media. Not because it's the worst thing keeping you stuck, but because if you're like me, it may be the most subtle thing.

I have a love/hate relationship with social media. It's how I make money. Some of you are reading this very book because you follow me on Facebook or Instagram or Pinterest.

Social media is what has opened soooooooo many doors for me, including collaborations with Hobby Lobby, meeting Dave Ramsey, speaking at events with Chip and JoJo Gaines (I am hoping that by calling her JoJo instead of Joanna, you will think we are tight. We are not, but a girl can hope), and so on. I have worked really, really hard to build an audience of over half a million followers, and I love getting to serve them.

But I've spent enough time online to understand that mindlessly scrolling through social media is killing more dreams and lives than people realize. As my friend Megan Tamte, owner of Evereve, says about scrolling, "You are watching other people's dreams come true at the expense of your own." In other words, as you scroll, scroll, and scroll some more, life is slipping you by. You're watching other people live, but you are stuck.

Mindlessly SCROLLING SOCIAL MEDIA *kills more* DREAMS AND LIVES THAN *people realize.*

My husband, Jason, is one of the only humans I know who is not on social media. And you guys, I have never seen anyone freer than he is.

Jason doesn't know our friends are out of the country . . . he's not on Instagram to see. He doesn't see the deep-sea fishing pics and froufrou drinks with umbrellas in them, so he feels zero jealousy. Zero anything. He doesn't know that so-and-so got a new car or new job or a new haircut or a new anything.

He's not aware of the sale that his favorite store is having, and he's not getting retargeting ads on his social media because our phones are always listening (#funnynotfunny).

He doesn't see all the courses that people are offering; therefore, he doesn't even know what he doesn't even know.

He isn't subjected to any news stories or opinions of others. He doesn't roll over in the morning and instantly check his DMs. He doesn't end his night mindlessly looking through the feed of his friend's neighbor's sister's dog's account on Instagram because he got off on some social rabbit trail.

Nope, he's just living his life.

He doesn't have the temptation of looking at his followers to determine his worth. And he doesn't need validation from anyone, and certainly not from people he doesn't see every day. He's not worrying about haters or the perfect Instagram angle. He leaves his phone on the nightstand or in the truck half the time, and although it drives me batty, I wish I had that same freedom.

Because by not being on social media . . . he really is free.

My friend, I am almost jealous of the freedom he has.

It's no wonder we are overwhelmed in our life when an article from Techjury.net says that adults are on social media an average of almost three hours a day . . . watching other people's lives.

Another study says an average person will spend more than five years of their lives on social media.[*] Five years! So whether it's three hours a day or five years of our lives, every day you and I are being inundated with people putting their "best face forward."

But this isn't just about watching other people on social. It's also about the pressure of putting our best life out there for others to see. We can become slaves to the selfies. I'm soooooo guilty of this, taking shot after shot until the light hits my face right and my double chin isn't showing and I look thinner than I actually am.

On a family vacation in Mexico recently, I was saddened to see how many people were spending more time *recording* their vacation than *experiencing it*. They were posing in the pool instead of playing in it and taking pictures of their fancy dinner plates instead of digging into the chips and salsa.

I am convinced that as a society, we've become more obsessed

---

[*] "How Much Time Do We Spend on Social Media?," Mediakix, https://mediakix .com/blog/how-much-time-is-spent-on-social-media-lifetime/.

with *looking* happy on social media than actually *being happy* in real life.

You can go to any big event, big concert, or preschool graduation, and person after person is filming the event. Social media has stolen our ability to be *in the moment* at the event because we are recording the moment to show we were there.

And then don't even get me started on the posting. All day every day, people are uploading the best version of themselves, in the perfect stance that looks like they are casually brushing the hair from their face. Yet I know it's taken them a professional photographer and at least ten attempts at that photo to get their best pose, all while showing you what amazing thing they have just bought, seen, or experienced.

We've become MORE OBSESSED WITH LOOKING HAPPY ONLINE THAN ACTUALLY *being happy* IN REAL LIFE.

You and I watch it like junkies, hour after hour, day after day, year after year, so it's no wonder we feel lesser than. When we are constantly bombarded with the best version of other people, and then look at our own hot mess, of course we don't measure up.

And those feelings of not measuring up keep us stuck.

We start to think "I have so far to go, is it even worth trying? I can never do it." Building a business from scratch. Losing thirty pounds. Whatever our particular challenge is, it's easy to end up believing "it's so far out there that it's not even worth the effort." We continue to stay stuck and living smaller than God ever intended for us to.

I suspect in my very core that we were more satisfied with our lives when we didn't know what anyone else was doing with theirs.

When we were oblivious to what we were missing out on. When instead of spending an hour pinning projects on Pinterest that I know full good and well I will never do, I was actually spending that time doing a project in real life with my kiddos.

And how addicted we are to social media is not your fault. I mean, signing in to your Instagram certainly is your fault, but social media has been set up in a way to make you want more and more of it even when you hate how it makes you feel.

Much of what you are getting on social media is *pressure*. It's subtle, but if you look for it, you will certainly find it.

Pressure to do it all.

Pressure to push harder.

Pressure to work more and hustle more.

Pressure to dream bigger and set bigger goals.

Pressure to "keep up with the Joneses."

Pressure to go places and be in the "group" or at the event.

It just never ends.

Friend, watching other people live their lives every day, for hours, will make you feel like you are never doing enough. Of course you feel overwhelmed.

I mentioned earlier how I stayed home when the kids were young. And I'm so thankful that social media wasn't even a thing then. Because during that season, I was called to peanut butter and jelly sandwiches with the crusts cut off and playing with LEGOs for the hundredth time every day. And the last thing that I needed would have been to see everyone I knew doing alllllll the things with alllllll the people. And I know me well enough to know, I would have spiraled into a "poor me" pit wondering if I was going to be stuck on diaper duty forever while all the people I followed on social media were out living the dream, living it up, with no baby puke stains on their clothing.

It would not have been good for me. I'm afraid I would have

had the kids on my lap but Instagram on my hand. I'm afraid I would have pushed to keep up on my career even though I knew God had it on hold for a season while I raised babies.

And while there are times that seeing what people are doing on social media is certainly inspiring, there are other times when it will cause you to take your eyes off your own life. There's a good reason the Bible tells us to "run with perseverance the race marked out for US" (Hebrews 12:1, capitals added). Because otherwise we will look around at all the other runners!

If you are constantly on social media, it's easy to question what you're doing and think it should be different or more. And that will make anyone overwhelmed.

We aren't all called to run a business or travel the world or start a revolution, you know. Some women are called to stay home full-time. Some women are called for a season to positions they wish they didn't have to be in (caring for aging parents, recovering from an illness, helping hurt children heal), and I hate that social media makes anyone second-guess what they are currently called to.

When I started rewriting this book for the third time, I decided to take a social media sabbatical, in part because I knew I didn't need the distraction of comparison. Sadly, when I saw other people's books, or big ideas, or success stories, I was starting to have moments of feeling lesser than.

I also knew that I didn't want the voice of social media to drown out the voice of God in my life. If I was gonna write the book God was asking me to, I had to somehow hear Him more clearly than I heard anyone else.

The social media sabbatical was a big deal for me. I've been on Facebook for ten years, and in all that time, I've never missed a single day of posting—not one—until God told me to sign off for two weeks. I knew I needed to write this book *my way* (by way of God's way), and in order to do that, I couldn't be distracted by what anyone else was doing. Sure, I twitched for a day or so, but man, did it feel soooooooo freeing after that.

If you've got a vision or a calling or a decision to make, you may need to protect yourself, friend. A "social sabbatical" may be just what the doctor ordered so you are not influenced by anyone but God Himself. Seeing all the things from all the people all the time is bound to influence your thoughts, your ideas, and your courage. You'll only twitch for a few days, I promise.

When I think about the idea of not watching everyone else, I think about how horses wear blinders when they're racing. Horses have peripheral vision, and left to their own devices, a horse will look around. And looking around on the racetrack, where a horse needs to be its best, can cause it to get distracted. The blinders keep them focused only on what's directly in front of them.

Friend, you don't need to be intimidated or distracted by what anyone else is doing. You have the God of the universe to show you how to do it right. And guess what? The things He shows you to do won't look exactly like what anyone else is doing. And being an original is so much better than being a carbon copy or a cheap knockoff of someone else and their life anyway.

> WHAT GOD *calls you* TO DO WON'T LOOK EXACTLY LIKE WHAT *anyone else* IS DOING.

Since returning to social, I've unfollowed a bunch of "influencers" and "successful people." And the reason I unfollowed them is not because of anything they were doing wrong, but because of how watching them *made me feel*.

I didn't like how I compared myself to them.

I didn't like how I felt jealous of their success.

I didn't like how I would start to wonder if I was doing things wrong because I was doing things differently.

I would tailspin and get stuck in my own head simply because watching them clouded my own vision.

Watching people who were where I wanted to be was making me have a hard time executing what God was asking *me* to do and who He was asking *me* to be. I was second-guessing what I thought God was asking me to do and *that's how I knew I needed a break. Because I needed a breakthrough.*

And so I took what Mark Zuckerberg has graciously offered to each of us . . . the unfollow button and the unfriend button, and I used them. And I suggest you consider doing the same.

Feeling stuck because of all you see on social media is not your fault. The apps were designed to make you want more, and I doubt we are ever going to see people posting "reality" over "really staged."

But, girl, if you are stuck and overwhelmed and scared, you gotta get a handle on how much you are on there and how much you are letting that mess influence you.

Social media is undoubtedly the distraction of our decade, perhaps of our generation. How many families do you see out for dinner and everyone is staring at their phone?

How many accidents are happening because of texting and driving?

We are distracted like never before.

Author and pastor Audrey Meisner says, "If the devil can't discourage you, he will do his best to distract you." Isn't that powerful?

My friend Caroline Kisler, who runs a childcare center, was even more direct. She posted one day, "What would happen if every time we went to log in to Facebook or Instagram, we hugged our kids instead?" Wow. That was a punch in the gut.

Social media is such a distraction.

And the bottom line is, when you are stuck, when you need

to make a shift or get the courage to try something new, you have zero capacity for distractions. What you are about to try to do is so outside of your comfort zone, that you can't afford to be distracted, my friend.

Sign off.

What you are about to try to do is going to require so much of you emotionally to rise above where you have been stuck that you can't risk being distracted.

Sign off.

What you are about to try is going to feel so vulnerable and so out of the norm for you, that if you are distracted while attempting it, you are likely to retreat.

Sign off, and then stay off too.

Let's talk about my social media sabbatical again. I have heard writers refer to the process of publishing a book as similar to the process of having a baby. So as I am "birthing" this new book thing, I feel so vulnerable.

And vulnerable feels like standing on the internet naked.

And so, as I am writing this book, it already feels like I'm in need of an epidural. I don't need the distraction of what pretty baby anyone else is birthing. I gotta focus on what God's got in front of me, and you gotta focus on what God has in front of you.

I double-dog dare you today to look at your social media usage and be super honest with yourself about your screen time. Is it helping to get you to where you want to go? Or is it keeping you stuck?

And if it's keeping you stuck, are you willing to go against what everyone else is doing and take a break? Just until you get over the hump of being stuck?

I read once that my imaginary BFF Joanna Gaines leaves her phone in her car when she gets home from work every day in order to limit distractions and focus fully on her family. It doesn't even get to come in the house. I cannot even imagine that. What a gift she is giving herself and her family.

Don't get stuck staring at social or letting social make you feel stuck.

Take it from someone who was just off for two weeks—you won't miss much. And you won't even know what you are missing.

So social media isn't making it any easier to get over your fear, but what about people? Are some people keeping you stuck? Let's address this in the next chapter.

chapter five

STUCK PEOPLE KEEP PEOPLE STUCK

Misery loves company,
but I keep ignoring the invites.
—UNKNOWN

I hopefully made my point that while I love being on social media, social media is not helping you get unstuck or past your fear.

And since I just got all up in your business in the last chapter, I want to talk about something else you are going to have to address if you are ever going to get unstuck and do things afraid.

A lot of us were handed the feelings of being stuck, scared, and overwhelmed pretty much at birth, or at least when we were young. Just like some people are born into and inherit wealth, you may have been born into and inherited struggle.

Some of the emotions and feelings you experience about doing hard things or making changes in your life are the result of how your mother or father did it. And how their mother or father did it before them. You may come from a long, long line of worriers, doubters, and people who have let fear control their lives.

What has been passed along to you from your parents or caregivers is not your fault.

So first of all, big hugs. If you have seen only very emotional, very weak, very stuck people and their decisions, it wasn't supposed to be that way.

But sadly, we often become the sum of what we have seen.

Your parents were stuck in financial struggles? Not surprised if you are too.

Your mom stayed stuck in bad relationships? It's no surprise you are doing it too.

If every time there was pressure in your family as a child, you saw your parents unravel, you can't expect to know how to handle pressure any differently than it was modeled to you.

I have a friend, Sue, who has become dear to our family. Sue helps keep our home running, and most exciting to me, she keeps my outside flowers and plants alive. (Insert all the praise hand emojis for live flowers and for Sue!)

Sue told me something the other day that broke my heart. Her mother died when she was very young, and her father remarried a woman who wasn't kind to her. Sue told me that her stepmother told her once that she should never wear the color red because it made her look fat. Sue is now sixty-three years old and has never worn anything red, other than when she had to wear it for work, which made her break down crying. She hates the color because of how wearing it triggers memories of how she was raised.

Friend, that breaks my heart. An entire color of the rainbow was ruined for Sue.

Now, I know wearing a color may not seem major, but it illustrates why things keep us stuck. Yes, some bad stuff has happened to us. But some of it was *put* on us.

Listen. Again, big hugs if you've been dealt a rough hand by people who should have done better by you. But we cannot as grown adults continue to let what people have put on us stick to us any longer. If we have any hope of living free lives, we have somehow got to break free of the junk they gave us.

Because some of what they gave you will literally steal, kill, and destroy you if you let it.

Even if you had a horrible experience or a horrific childhood, you can only blame your past for so long and then it's time to take some responsibility.

I've already told you about how I left home right out of high school and have supported myself ever since. I say that half with pride and half with irritation that my parents did not help me. Apparently I was a little bitter about that, and it all came back up last year when Jason and I were finishing off the basement in our new home.

I was talking with our builder, David, who mentioned that he was helping one of his daughters renovate her home.

I felt a little triggered. And by triggered, I mean jealous. I said something like, "Wow, how great for your daughter. My parents have never paid for anything." I went on to tell him how it pained me that I paid for college and most of our wedding and all our homes.

"Well, Jennifer," David said, "your dad gave you an even better gift. Look at what you've built here. Your dad gave you the gift of having to do it all on your own, and that is a better gift than giving you money."

I felt sucker punched. He was right.

You see, for years I'd felt resentment that my parents did well financially and had the means to help me but chose not to. But David reframed that burden into a gift. I had never looked at it from that angle.

Everything comes down to perception, my friend.

Maybe you still hate what was handed to you. And possibly with good reason.

But maybe if you can reframe it, you'll see it has actually made you who you are today.

Let me help you with a few more reframes.

If all you have seen is your mom make terrible decisions in relationships, well, hopefully now you have the gift of discernment. You know what not to do.

If you were handed chaos, hopefully you see the gift of living in peace and do that.

If you were handed financial struggles, and all you knew was things being tight and hard and barely scraping by, I bet now you know how to work, and I bet you appreciate all you have in a way others don't.

> WHAT YOU WERE HANDED IS NOT YOUR *handicap*; IT CAN BE YOUR *secret sauce*.

I want to make it very clear that whatever generational junk you were dealt, you don't have to keep it, claim it, or pay for it any longer.

You are not them.

Their mistakes are not your inheritance.

You don't have to repeat what you saw and what you experienced.

I know you may have been dealt a rotten hand, but you can change the whole game if you want to. And I can't wait to see you do it.

Think about it like this: you don't need more than what you have or anything different to do what God is asking you to do. Because if you needed something different, God would have already given it to you.

What you were handed is not your handicap; it can be your secret sauce. It's your competitive advantage. It's maybe even your blessing in disguise . . . *if* you choose to view it in that way.

I look back on all the heartache in my life—my daddy issues, the broken family, the miscarriages, the marriage struggles, the lost jobs, the robbery, the people who walked away—and with absolute certainty, I know that had I not gone through all that, I could never write this.

So yes, some of why you are stuck is because of what you have seen and what's been handed to you. But reframing how you look at your past will hopefully help you get unstuck despite your fear.

But what about the stuff people are trying to hand you *now*?

Ohhhhhhhhh, girl, this one is a doozie.

When a woman is trying to get unstuck or get past being overwhelmed and her fear, there are all too often people close to her, even people she loves, trying to sink her before she can sail.

This is something I have become hyperaware of, especially as my platform has grown and my business has exploded. Not everyone is for me. Even people close to me, whom I think *should* be in my corner, aren't always.

And here's what I've learned: girl, you aren't for everyone.

You aren't supposed to be.

Even Jesus had haters, for goodness' sake.

But I do think it's important to understand that there is a big difference between a hater and someone who's just trying to keep you stuck so that they feel better about their own life.

A hater says, "You aren't good enough to move into that apartment." But someone wanting to keep you stuck says, "You'll probably act too good for us now that you're moving into that fancy apartment."

See the difference? It's a subtle, manipulative, backhanded plea asking you not to change. No thank you.

A person may mom-shame you and ask who's gonna watch the kids if you go to a hotel to write your book for the weekend (#truestory). They may "jokingly" talk about how you don't have time for them anymore. They may suddenly begin to phase you out of their life as punishment for you wanting and doing and getting more (#alsoatruestory). Bye, Felicia.

Many people are coasting through life on autopilot, and for them to be near someone like you, who wants more and is trying for more, is going to be hard. Sometimes it's because of jealousy. Often it's because of fear. Sometimes it's because you are just too much for them.

Some people who "knew you when" don't want you to forget where you came from. Ever. They will remind you of your every shortcoming, every bad decision, and every failure. They will make comments on your Facebook page about that time you failed miserably back in 1989. Oh yes, they'll go back that far.

Family or old friends who are triggered by your success will ask, either out loud or through their body language, "Who do you think you are?" They'll act like you've got an attitude or are on some high horse.

Please know that this isn't a reflection of whether they love you. They probably do. But they're probably also struggling with being stuck themselves because they are broken people. You have probably heard that hurt people, hurt people. Well, it's also true that broken people break people. And stuck people keep people stuck with them. They don't want you to change or do better, because that convicts them of things they may not want to see in their own life. Your growing reminds them that they should be digging deep and making changes too. Your changing threatens the future of your relationship. They might worry that if you change, your relationship with them will change (and it probably will). They fear you will look at them differently (and you probably will). They fear you won't have time for them (and you may not). Even if they don't realize it, their fear causes them to say and do things to try to hold you back with them.

Of course, you and I both know that you trying something new has nothing to do with you thinking you're better than them. You wanting more for yourself does not mean you think less of them.

Friend, whatever they're dishing your way has so little to do with you and everything to do with them. And you need to run, not walk, from those saboteurs in your life.

At some point you have to get serious enough about your life that Aunt Linda's opinion about you switching jobs doesn't matter. You need to get sold out enough on believing God is asking you to make a change that it doesn't matter if Susie at work is posting passive-aggressive memes on Facebook to take a dig at you.

For real. That is toxic junk that will keep you stuck and playing small forever.

I'm not telling you to ditch your family or friends, but I am telling you to use great wisdom in who you share things with. Avoid sharing things with the dream crushers. Because they are the ones who will lead you off track.

When you're working to get un-stuck, stick with unstuck people. They are the free ones, and their freedom is contagious.

"But Jennifer, what if it's my husband who's not supporting my dream?"

Every now and then, a woman will ask me this question. She is stuck, over-whelmed, and scared to do things she feels called to do, but it's her spouse who's not on board with her making changes to their life.

Stuck **PEOPLE WILL TRY TO KEEP PEOPLE STUCK** *with them.*

Warning, my advice is not popular with some people, and it may not be what you want to hear, but it is biblical, so here we go: you can't ignore the opinions or the position of the man you promised till death do you part.

Psalm 133 says that where there is unity, blessing will follow. So if you're married, it's important for your husband to be in agreement with what you're doing. You want his buy-in. And if you don't have it, then it's time to pause and pray.

I know it's tempting to want to throw a hissy fit (I am guilty) or pressure him (guilty too) or even try to punish him, but I encourage you not to. That won't change his heart.

Girl, give him over to God. Sic the Holy Spirit on him. Ask God to change his heart and make him see things in a different light. Because conviction from God is always so much better than anything that comes from you.

What does this look like? First, it means you talk to God about your concerns and not to your girlfriends. God can change your husband's heart; your girlfriends can't.

Second, give him time. And give God time. Sometimes your husband just may need some time to digest this new idea you're throwing at him. If you're like me, you are never short on new ideas. Poor Mr. Magic—the name my social media followers dubbed Jason back in the days my business was called The Magic Brush—gets hit with new ideas on the daily. Bless his heart.

Third, make sure you're supporting your husband in the things that are important to him. You can't say no to his dreams and expect him to support yours. That's called hypocrisy.

That also means you can't tell him no in other areas of life that are important to him just to punish him, and then expect his yes to things that matter to you. It's called bedroom ministry, sis, but that's another book.

Your husband knows you better than anyone else, and often he has a perspective that you don't. He may be looking at the dollars or time it's going to cost or the emotional investment of whatever you want to do, and he just doesn't see how it can work out. It's wise of you to honor that. I'm not saying it's fun or it's comfortable, but it is right. And when we give honor where honor is due, God honors us.

But friend, if your marriage situation is a hot stinkin' mess that goes way beyond a lack of enthusiasm for a specific decision, get help. Call your pastor. Call a therapist. Like, yesterday. Don't keep calling your friend Lisa to gripe about your husband. Lisa can't fix this. But getting help for yourself and counsel on how to handle the decision-making process in your marriage is money and time well spent.

But at the end of the day, you work on you and you let God work on him. Because when you have your husband's blessing on what you are doing, *everything changes*. The possibilities and the potential are endless. You *want* to be on the same page, because when you are, that is power-couple stuff right there.

So listen, some of the reason you are still stuck could very well be that you haven't had a good example of what a free woman looks like. You need to see one. Find one in real life or on social media if it's a last resort. But study her. See how she rises above. See how when others go low, she goes high (thank you, Michelle Obama).

Watch how she is trying to do things afraid and refuses to stay stuck. Observe how she handles things that would terrify you. See how she demonstrates grace under fire.

Girl, whatever you have been through and whatever people say to you, don't use it as an excuse. Use it as an incentive to get out and get on with your life.

I'm cheerleading so hard for you right now, because even though it isn't all your fault, it *is* your responsibility.

And I know some of you are so broken and so tired of being stuck that you are willing to do anything to make a change.

And changing your mind is the first step to changing your life.

Now listen, the next chapter gets my blood pressure way up. I gotta slow my roll because my fingers are typing way too fast and my eye-brows are all up in a way that gives me wrinkles, and Botox is expensive.

If you think you need confidence to change your mind and change your life, there is no need to read the next chapter, 'cuz you won't get it there.

But you will get what you need. And it's straight-up truth, friend. Keep reading!

chapter six

CONFIDENCE IS NOT THE GOAL

*Courage is being scared to death
but saddling up anyway.*
—JOHN WAYNE

We've determined that social media is stacked against you.

And sometimes your upbringing and family and the people around you are holding you back.

But you know what else is keeping you stuck? The world's message of *confidence*.

If I had a dollar for every woman I meet who says she wishes she were more confident, I would be a rich, rich woman.

Over and over, I hear women say that they are waiting to do the next right or big thing until they feel more confident. They think that confidence is the magic, secret ingredient that makes everything better and will get them unstuck and moving forward.

As if.

"I'm not confident enough yet to start charging for my painting," they tell me. Or, "I don't have the confidence yet to start blogging." Or, "I wish I was confident enough to leave my day job."

Every time I hear that, I cringe. What does confidence have to do with anything? If they are waiting for confidence, they may be waiting forever.

I'm gonna have to simmer down a bit as I write this because it just fills me with a righteous anger on your behalf. The influencers, the personal development coaches, and the social media gurus who are all selling you confidence are lying to you.

IF YOU'RE WAITING FOR *confidence*, YOU MAY BE WAITING *forever*.

Oh, it's not out of malice. They're lying because they don't know any better. (Or maybe they *do* know better, but let's give them the benefit of the doubt.)

The first lesson of business is, "Sell them what they want and then give them what they need." And since everyone these days wants to be confident, the marketers are selling it left and right.

There are people teaching courses about confidence, and writing books about confidence, and making money hand over fist on the idea of confidence *because confidence sells*. How to get confident, how to feel confident, how to look confident.

Every day I coach women who are stuck and overwhelmed, and they tell me they're waiting for confidence. As if confidence is their magic pill. As if confidence will fix all their big feelings. As if confidence will ride in like a knight in shining armor to save the day.

As if it's even possible for confidence to magically appear at a given point in time, like there's a "confidence clock" counting down somewhere.

They ask, "Jen, how did you get the confidence to write a book proposal or to host your first conference or to speak on a stage in front of two thousand people?"

My only answer is that in those moments, I was not confident at all. How could I possibly be confident of something I had never done before?

It would be insane if, before our kids could walk, we expected them to feel confident about walking, right? It would be insane to expect my son to feel confident about filling out college applications when he's never done it before.

Which leads me to a conclusion that, while not very popular, I believe to be 100 percent truth:

Confidence is crap. Confidence is not what we should shoot for or wait on. *Confidence is not the goal.*

The definition of *confidence*, according to my friend Google, is "a feeling of self-assurance arising from one's appreciation of one's own abilities or qualities."

Read that again, and this time look at all the ways confidence is focused on self and one's own abilities. As a Christian, that just doesn't sit well with me. Focus on self is always a dead-end.

This summer, we took my parents on our family vacation to Mexico, because for the first time in our lives, we could afford to take them. (But also, we have a ton of kids, and tons of kids need tons of help.)

My kids' favorite thing to do on any vacation is to go zip-lining. Which is basically to say they enjoy being suspended in the air, sliding across a cable, and giving their mom a heart attack by dangling upside down over a jungle every chance they get in foreign countries. Lovely.

So while we were in Cancun, we found a zip-line course over the jungle. When we got to the course, I honestly wasn't sure if my mom and stepdad would zip-line with us or not. After all, my mom is sixty-eight years young, and she has a huge fear of heights. She's the woman on the plane snapping her wrist with a rubber band in order to calm her nerves. My mom has amazing qualities and can bake like Betty Crocker herself, but a flier she is not.

The tallest tower at the zip-line course was ninety-five feet tall, and that's about 765,478,985,852 steps to the top in the heat of summer.

If my mom had said no to the idea of zip-lining, I would not have blamed her. But she didn't. She climbed all seven towers and did all seven zip lines with the rest of us, and she enjoyed every single second of it. And no one was more shocked and more proud than I was.

Of course, we recorded video clips and took all the photos, because if it isn't on social media, did it even really happen? After my mom posted her pics, one of her Facebook friends commented, "Connie, I can't believe you zip-lined!"

My mom answered, "Well, they didn't give you any time to think about it. They had me strapped in and walking off the ledge before I even had time to consider it."

And that wisdom from my mom, my friend, is one major key to getting the confidence you want.

Mom didn't have time to think about it. She just did it. She didn't plan. She didn't consider. She didn't ponder. She didn't make a list of pros and cons. She didn't call all four of her closest girlfriends to get their opinions. And most of all, she didn't over-think it.

I wonder how powerful you and I would be if we applied my mom's zip-lining strategy to every area of our life?

What would happen if every time an opportunity presented itself that you feel like you want to do or are supposed to do . . . what would happen if you didn't think, but just did?

I wonder how much more powerful we could be, how much more effective for our purpose and for the kingdom of God we could be, if we didn't stop to rationalize things that are put in front of us every.single.time.

Wondering about going back to school? No need to do a pros-and-cons list. Just call the admissions office for info today.

WHAT WOULD HAPPEN IF YOU DIDN'T *think*, BUT JUST *did?*

Thinking about asking out that guy in your singles group? No need to keep thinking. Send him a DM today and see what he says.

We have become a society of over-thinkers. News flash: not everything needs to be thought about. You are giving your mind too much time to rationalize and talk yourself out of things.

If you just look at my mom's Face-book photos, she looks totally confident up there on the platform, getting ready to soar over the jungle of Mexico. But her reality was totally different. She didn't stop being scared of heights. She wasn't full of self-assurance in her own abilities. She just jumped anyway.

Many of the people who look like they have "made it" have incredible insecurities and fear. That day I was onstage with Chip and Joanna Gaines? #thoughtiwoulddie.

I wasn't onstage because I was *confident*. I was onstage because I was *obedient*. God opened a door and I said yes. I had the courage to say yes, and whether or not I had confidence was not even a factor.

The only difference between you and that girl who has 10,000 followers on her health and wellness Facebook page is that one day she woke up and said, "I may not know everything, but I am starting the page anyway."

The only thing that is different between you and the girl who is getting that promotion that you've wanted for the last decade is that she woke up one day and decided it didn't matter how old she was or what anyone thought of her decision, and she applied for it.

You think people are confident, but no . . . they just have *courage*.

Courage should be our goal, friend.

In this world of Instagram selfies and online marketing, lots of people are faking confidence. They are staging pics of themselves dangling off the side of staircases and mindlessly tipping their hats and hoping their pictures reek of confidence. They're acting out that whole "fake it 'til you make it" scenario that they think will attract followers and customers and friends.

Side note: I don't know about you, but personally, I would rather someone tell me they have no stinkin' clue what they are doing. Faking it is for charades and other games, and ain't nobody got time for that in the year 2020.

Life is too short to be faking anything except eyelashes and plants.

Several years ago, Jason got me the book called *Crash the Chatterbox* by Steven Furtick. Pastor Steven is one of my absolute favorite authors, a master communicator who helps me understand the Bible, and I highly recommend you listen to his podcast or follow him on social.

Crash the Chatterbox was such a game changer for me that it's now recommended reading for every person in my business group. This is the book that helped me understand that we *all* have "imposter syndrome," that internal voice that speaks negative and self-defeating thoughts.

Imposter syndrome is the nagging thought that at any moment, everyone will see you are a fraud. Despite your accomplishments, despite your accolades, despite the evidence, you are certain that at any moment, the world will find out you don't really know what you are doing and it's all going up in flames.

Steven's book was so helpful because it taught me how to recognize the voices in my own head. I can be my own worst enemy. And it basically convinced me that no one, and I mean *no one*, is exempt from feeling inadequate sometimes.

The truth is that so many of the people who appear for all practical purposes to be "successful" aren't always confident. Or ever confident, for that matter. They just do things *in spite of* their confidence level.

Here's the thing, my friend: confidence is an end result, the byproduct, and the happy consequence of doing things while you're afraid. *While you are afraid.*

Confidence is what comes *after* you do the thing that you are scared of, and then do the thing again, and then do the thing again.

Confidence has to be earned. It's an accumulation over time. There's no shortcut to confidence, and anyone who tells you different is trying to sell you something. The truth is, the only way to gain confidence is through experience. You can't buy it, manifest it, package it, or wish it into existence.

The reason you're stuck isn't because you lack confidence. No, you're lacking the experience that will help you *feel* confident. It's such a huge difference.

But I need you to quit waiting for confidence before you get out of your rut and out of your head. You don't need confidence. You just need the guts and the courage to say yes to something even with that nervous feeling in the pit of your belly.

Are you catching what I'm throwing here?

You do not need confidence. You need *courage*.

Courage is "the ability to do something that frightens one." (Thanks, Google.) See the difference? It's not a feeling.

Courage means you do what's necessary to make things happen, regardless of your feelings or confidence in a matter.

Courage will push you way outside your comfort zone. Courage will have you signing up for classes and applying for jobs and making a website to announce the launch of your own business before confidence ever comes into the equation.

Courage will have you trying one final round of IVF even though your heart has been broken before. Courage will have you running for city council even though you lost last time. Courage will even lead you to zip-line for the first time in your life at age sixty-eight.

Courage is willing to take risks when you don't know how it's gonna work out.

Courage is rolling the dice on a hopeful outcome because there are no guarantees that the thing you are going to do is going to work out or be a success.

Courage says, I DON'T KNOW WHAT I'M DOING, BUT I'LL TRY IT ANYWAY.

Courage is what will make you say yes to things in spite of your feelings about it.

Confidence says, *I know what I'm doing.* Courage says, *I don't know what I'm doing, but I'll try it anyway.*

Confidence says I know what I am capable of. Courage says I know *who* makes me capable.

Confidence boasts. Courage listens.

Confidence says I can do it. Courage says I'm not sure if I can do it, but I'm willing to try.

Confidence says I've done this before, so I feel good about it. Courage says I am willing to begin.

Confidence operates from a place of personal power. Courage operates from a place of personal conviction.

Confidence thinks I can handle anything thrown at me. Courage knows that I can turn to others for help to handle what's thrown at me.

Confidence focuses on self. Courage focuses on what needs to be done.

Confidence is the result of courage in action.

Motivational blogger Yunzhe Zhou says, "Courage is thriving under uncertainty while confidence is the assessment afterwards."

As I write this, I have finished ten triathlons. I can now say with confidence that if I do an 11th or 111th triathlon, I feel pretty confident that I will finish and will not die.

Did I have this same confidence at the first race? No. Did I have this confidence at the second race? Nope. At the time, I was convinced that not dying the first time had been a total fluke. Did I have this confidence by the third race? Perhaps. Perhaps by the third time, I was feeling a tiny bit more confident.

Am I still scared every time? Absolutely. Do I still panic every time? You bet your britches I do. (And by "panic," I mean gasping for breath on a lifeguard's rescue buoy every.stinkin'.time.)

But I had *courage* to sign up. And my past experience of not dying ten times would tell me that I can rely on that experience to conclude that I can be confident about not dying. I'm still not a confident swimmer, but I am confident that I will finish.

But what if I'd waited to feel confident before I signed up for that first race? I would still be waiting. Instead, I gathered the courage to sign up, and the confidence came over time.

Here's another gem from Instagram, quoting Daniel Maher: "Confidence is courage at ease."

I would like to think that when I feel called to do something out of my comfort zone that my confidence in myself doesn't matter. I may not feel qualified or assured of my own abilities, but I am confident in the One who did the asking.

That's the difference between self-confidence and confidence in God. Self-confidence puts all my focus on my own abilities. Having confidence in God means I believe He is who He says He is, and He will do what He says He will do. And if He is calling me *to* it, He will certainly call me *through* it. And I can have confidence in all that!

Self-confidence is a word that sells, but confidence in the Lord is where I am willing to put all my chips any day of the week.

You see, God will never tap you on the shoulder and ask you to do something that He can't 100 percent equip you to do. The Bible says He will equip those He calls (2 Corinthians 9:8).

Confidence IS THE RESULT OF COURAGE IN ACTION.

God knows that you are representing Him. People are watching you live out your life. Why would He set you up for failure? That would make Him look bad!

The pressure is not on you to perform. The only pressure is on you to have courage to say yes, and then it's on God to provide. Confidence may or may not come. But that's not the point.

I don't know about you, but I know that if I give myself too long to think about things, I can talk myself out of about anything. Maybe you know what I'm talking about. I can give myself the laundry list of reasons why I should not attempt the big, hard, and scary thing.

That "talk myself out of it" voice has convinced me more often than not that I should not get up off the sofa and take a jog, so I know that voice isn't always on my side. But still, human nature is to protect ourselves from things that are hard, so that is why we talk ourselves out of things.

It's natural and easy to say no to hard things and say yes to easy things. So one of the things I've found that helps me to act with courage is to find other people to be courageous with. My mom would never have zip-lined solo. She did it because we were all with her.

FOMO (fear of missing out) is a real thing, you all. So if you're facing something big, call a couple of girlfriends and invite them to join you.

Doing things alone always feels more exposed. The vulnerability factor is so much higher and no one likes to feel vulnerable. If you get people to do something with you, you'll have accountability and someone to urge you forward, because let's be honest. When others are with you, you will want to keep up because no one wants to look like a punk, #amiright?

Plus, courage is contagious. You can't be around brave people and not eventually have it wear off on you. This is why *who* is in your circle is so important. As I tell my kids, show me your friends and I'll show you your future. So consider the people around you carefully, including the people you interact with online. You cannot listen to complainers and blamers and Debbie Downers day in and day out and think you will make positive, courageous decisions.

As I write this book, my dear girlfriends Carrie and Laura are fasting and praying on my behalf, for several days in a row. Why? They are confident of God's call on my life. They know this book will break chains and help set women free. And they believe in that enough to sacrifice their time and their full bellies to help bring it to fruition. What a gift they are to me! What a treasure on this side of heaven! I can't thank them enough.

These are the type of women you want rooting for you and in your corner, the ones who believe in you even when *you* are not confident yet.

I love the saying from Jim Rohn that says, "You are the average of the five people you spend the most time with."

So girl, get around people who will encourage you regardless of your confidence level. And if you're still struggling with getting enough courage to say yes to things in your life? Set aside some time just to remember. Stop and think about all the times when God has come through for you in the past. This can be hard for me as an Enneagram 3 (always moving on to the next thing), with menopause brain and a bad memory. But I've learned to hunt up my old journals and photo albums to help me remember the times when I have prayed and God has answered, giving me courage to try something.

I know the world is telling you to journal daily so that you can "manifest what you want out of life." I know you're being told to write down everything you want to see happen for yourself. Write down your goals, write what you're gonna do to meet them, and so on.

Well, that's great, but how about you journal the things God has *already* done for you? Instead of what you *want*, how about you remember what He's already *done*? Boom! #micdrop.

Rereading the stories of the times He's come through or made a way will remind you that He brought you through already. You'll remember the times you gathered your courage and acted even though you were scared, and you *didn't die*. Remember those times!

I once saw a sign in Seaside, Florida—one of my favorite places—that had me diving for my phone to take a picture. The sign said simply, "God, give me guts."

Oh, that's so gritty. That's so meaty. Talking about confidence feels precious. But guts . . . I think that *guts is courage with clothes on*. It's a mountain mover. And it just sounds bad to the bone.

So I'm gonna pray right now for every woman reading this book that God would give you guts.

Give you guts to make the phone call you need to make. Give you guts to shut your mouth when you'd rather run it. Give you guts to launch the next thing. Give you guts to rest even when there are a million things still on your list. Give you guts to have that hard conversation. Give you guts to walk away. Lord, give her guts!

Yes, this kind of courage will require something of you, and you won't always be confident of the outcome. Courage is most often shown, unfortunately, when we are knee-deep in the trenches without the slightest idea of what's ahead.

If you're stuck, pray for courage, my friend. Or if it feels better, pray for guts.

And it's time, right here at the end of this chapter, to stop telling yourself that you're stuck, and instead muster up the courage to do what God is asking you to do or what the desires in your heart are leading you toward. I double-dog dare you.

I know the world is chatting about confidence all day, every day, making you think you have to feel confident before you do anything big. But you can start doing something courageous today, and trust that confidence will come later. You can get better at whatever you do if you don't rob yourself of the opportunity to start.

As the Chinese proverb says, the journey of a thousand miles begins with a single step.

It's time. It's time to get unstuck, out of your head, and living the life you are meant to. What is God asking you to be courageous about today?

chapter seven

BUT MAYBE, PERHAPS, SUPPOSEDLY, STAYING STUCK IS KINDA, SORTA YOUR FAULT

The price of inaction is far greater
than the cost of a mistake.

—MEG WHITMAN

I hope you got warm fuzzies in that last chapter. You're feeling all courageous to get unstuck and we're friends now, right? Because now it's time to discuss something that *is* probably your fault when it comes to staying stuck and playing small because of fear: owning your own junk.

This one may sting a bit more, but it's important, because owning your junk and accepting personal responsibility for what you have done in the past and continue to do in the present and future, is so big.

I want you to know that change is possible for your life, but it's entirely up to you. You, and you alone, are responsible for how you handle whatever you were handed in life and how you handle both yourself and your emotions *today*.

But first, let's talk about elephants.

Do you know how trainers control elephants? When elephants are born into captivity, trainers control them by tying them to a tree, fence post, or something else that can hold them.

Initially, the baby elephant pulls at the rope and tries to break free. But elephants are quitters. They give up fighting for freedom pretty quickly when they realize they are unable to get loose.

Eventually, elephants grow and mature and get so big that they could easily break the rope, but something crazypants happens. They don't even try. And it's not because the trainers use heavier ropes or bigger trees. In fact, as an elephant gets older and bigger, trainers are able to use a *smaller* rope and *smaller* things to keep the animals tied up.

That's because something has happened *in the mind* of the elephant. It still believes it's stuck. It has been conditioned to believe it cannot break free, so it doesn't even try.

This truth slays me. The elephant could be free and doesn't even know it. And what's true for those elephants is also true for people.

We think we are stuck when we are *so close* to freedom!

Among the women I coach in my business, there are so many SRPs just like me, who for most of their lives have been serving others to the degree that they have not even considered what it is that *they* want from life. They are stuck.

There are women who have stuffed down their dreams and aspirations so far that they have determined it's not even possible to see those dreams come to pass in this lifetime. They are stuck.

There are women who are so beat down by life and so far into survival mode that they don't dare to dream again, because dreaming feels like a setup for disappointment. Dreaming feels dangerous, and smart people avoid danger at all costs. Amiright?

I also see many women who get to a certain age (the actual number doesn't matter, but it's a magic line they conjured in their own mind) and decide that they missed their window. They decide that this is all they can expect from life. They may be in pain, desperate for more, broke, sick, unhappy, or broken, but they resolve to themselves that getting by, day to day, is all that is available to them. I call this "dead women walking." They are stuck.

I see women who have made mistakes (haven't we all?) and they believe that "just barely getting by" is their life sentence for those mistakes. Oh sis, God has so much more in store for you.

I see women who want to stay home and raise their kids who feel shamed by others into thinking something must be wrong with them, that they should want something in addition to the title "Mom."

That's a bunch of baloney. There are so many women whose deepest dream is to be home. Please do not let social media tell you what "wanting more" should look like. It's not always a six-figure salary. It's not always rocking a stage. It's not always taking over the world. For years, I wanted nothing more than daily naps with my babies. And I got them, and I will never regret that.

I meet so many women who are feeling stuck in their lives, unable to move toward the thing that they want and the thing that God calls them to, because they have tied their minds to a false truth.

> DO NOT LET *social media* TELL YOU WHAT "WANTING MORE" SHOULD *look like*.

Often they are tying themselves to the person they were in their past. They are keeping themselves stuck because they just won't let things go. They won't let go of old ways of thinking. They won't let go of old habits. They won't let go of old people.

They are only stuck because they are continuing to *choose* stuck on a daily basis.

We, like elephants, have the strength to break free from the flimsy ropes that are holding us in place, but too often we have grown comfortable in our stuckness. We carry it around like a toddler's favorite blanket. Because when we are terrified, it's easier to claim, "I'm stuck" than it is to gather courage and say, "I'm trying again."

Friend, what you are doing, the words you are using, the wrong thought patterns that you are playing over and over in your mind, they are not serving you well. And in order to get you from stuck to free, we have to be able to recognize our own stinkin' thinkin' (thank you, Joyce Meyer, for that terminology). Let me give you an example.

As a mom, I show love to my kids by helping them see when they're acting like knuckleheads. And real love is helping them work through why they do what they do so they don't do it again.

For example, one of my kids has a friend who is totally flaky. There is just no other way to say it. They say they will come over and do not. They make plans and then cancel, or worse, just don't show. They dump plans with my kiddo if a better offer comes up.

As a mom, it makes me want to say, "Hold my earrings." Can I get a witness?

One day I told my child that they needed to stand up for themself with this friend. But even as I was talking, God reminded me that I have never been good at letting people know when I'm not okay with how they treat me. I have stayed in relationships, both personal and professional, that I shouldn't have, and have always had trouble standing up for myself. I generally make decisions that keep the peace and don't ruffle any feathers. Peace at all costs has always been my go-to emotion.

And then it hit me . . . oh my gosh, my kiddo is acting just like me!

In fact, one of the reasons this manuscript was hard for me to write is because I wanted to be bolder in my writing. I wanted to write the things that I know to be truth, even if I don't have the courage to say those same things out loud.

I am praying God will give me that grace, but I'm not there yet. I might sound cocky on paper, but I still struggle with hard conversations. I can shrink down and behave like a wounded middle schooler in a hot second. I don't say what I so badly want to for fear of upsetting people. And now I have to ask myself, is my son doing the same thing? Is he not telling his friend that his feelings are hurt, or that standing him up is not okay, because of me? Did I hand my son "being a pushover"? Did I hand him "just take it"? Because that isn't okay. That is NOT what I want to hand any of my children.

These kind of *aha* moments will change your life if you let them.

When God shows you how you are behaving and then is kind enough to lovingly show you *why* you behave in that way, it is a game changer.

This, my friend, will get you unstuck.

I need for you to understand that you are not defined by the awful things that happened to you. That traumatic childhood, that abusive boyfriend, that cheating spouse, that friend who betrayed you . . . those experiences are not *all* of you. Certainly, a part of you, but not all of you.

They are not who you are.

You are a grown woman, capable of healing, capable of being whole, capable of doing hard things, capable of moving forward. God does not mark your life by one event or tragedy or a series of them, for that matter, and you should not either.

It's time to stop replaying the old tapes and the old mistakes over and over in your mind. You are not who you were back then.

You aren't who you were last month. You are not even the same person you were yesterday if you did any sort of reflection, prayer, or anything to grow yourself in the last twenty-four hours.

You may have failed, but you are not a failure. You don't have to stay stuck. Try again.

That bad relationship you stayed in would never happen with the person you are today. That bad business deal was just that. It was bad. But you learned. And now you know what *not* to do.

You may HAVE FAILED, BUT YOU ARE *not a failure.*

Yes, you messed up and flunked out of school. Yes, you went bankrupt one time, but now you know better. And when you know better, you do better.

You are capable of getting unstuck if you change how you think about what you already did.

One of my favorite movies is *The Shawshank Redemption*, about a group of inmates in prison. Even though their incarceration is difficult and painful, to the inmates it becomes familiar, even almost comfortable. I would think that inmates in a place like Shawshank would want to be released, but the movie shows many of them struggling when they get a taste of freedom. Being locked up has become the thing that feels safest.

Just like the elephants.

Just like you and me.

Did you catch that?

The way we act and react to things and the way we think about what we have been through is what ties us down and keeps us stuck. We *say* we want to be free, but our behavior often tells on us.

Can you relate to these habits:

Do you get completely stuck in your own head? You're choosing to stay stuck.

Are you an overthinker? Do you think things to death? And

the more you consider things, the more stuck you are? You're choosing to stay stuck.

Is it hard to get out of your own way because you are your own worst enemy? Who needs haters when your own terrible self-talk is self-loathing? Girl, quit. Your words are keeping you stuck.

Are you self-sabotaging? As soon as you gain a little momentum, do you shoot yourself in the foot, like my friend Carrie who canceled her Facebook ad? You know when you do this, don't you? You know when you stop yourself from leaning in the direction of freedom.

Do you use the excuse that you are too shy, too weird, or too old or too young or too whatever to do things that are out of your comfort zone? I love you, but that's lame. What God asks you to do, the desires He puts in your heart, you are *already* equipped for. And if you aren't, He'll bring people alongside you who are. But that's a whole different book.

Do you get so jealous of others and spend so much time comparing yourself to them that you get stuck?

Are you waiting to do things until you are perfect? Oh friend, I have a story coming up for you.

Are you harboring unforgiveness and bitterness? Oh, I've got a whole *chapter* on this coming for you, girlfriend.

Listen, there *is* stuff beyond our control. How we were raised, the things we were handed from our parents, the things we see on social media. But keeping yourself tied to false beliefs, wrong thinking, and excuses *is* all your fault. And mine.

And the good news is, this is *fixable*.

The reason we stay tied to excuses is because we are scared. And unless you are Wonder Woman, you *will* get scared at times.

We all feel fear.

And it's human nature not to want to do the thing in front of us or the thing God is asking us to do or the thing we think we are supposed to do because we know it will be *hard*. And *scary*.

So we self-protect by making up all the reasons why we can't.

Girl, you are not alone. I hear dozens, maybe hundreds, of "I am scared" statements every single day. In my emails. In my DMs. In my paid coaching groups.

I'm scared I will fail.

I'm scared I will succeed and have to keep it up.

I'm scared I won't be able to handle success.

I'm scared it will change me.

I'm scared people will treat me differently.

I'm scared they'll find out I don't know what I'm doing.

I'm scared I'll go too fast.

I'm scared I'll go too slow.

I'm scared I'll look bad.

I'm scared I'll make a mistake.

I'm scared it will hurt my family.

I'm scared my kids will resent me.

I'm scared I'll end up broke.

I'm scared I'm not smart enough.

Friend, any time you are trying to do something you have not done before, something that feels big to you (because what feels big, hard, and scary to me may be an area that is not a big deal for you), or something that takes you out of your comfort zone, you *will* feel scared.

We were designed to feel fear when faced with something that feels threatening.

Standing on the edge of a cliff, you should feel fear. It will save you from jumping.

Staring into the face of a lion, you should feel fear. It will provoke you to run to save your life.

Your brain is literally trying to save you from the pain of

being uncomfortable. It's trying to save you from the pain of doing something you don't have experience with. It's flashing a warning light and waving its arms frantically at you, warning you that you might die if you don't pay attention.

But your brain lies to you.

Your feelings lie to you.

Starting a website will not kill you. Going back to college is not a threat. Taking baby steps toward adoption is not a bad thing. Moving towns is not permanent. Starting a business is not as hard as you think.

Your brain is instinctively trying to protect you from doing the big, hard, and scary things that can free you.

And listen, I am not a doctor or a therapist and don't want to even begin to pretend I know how your brain works. But I know this:

God can fix bad thinking.

God can show you how your mind is keeping you from your freedom.

God can point out in a way that only He can how you are your own worst enemy when it comes to getting unstuck.

Trust me, I know. I have an overactive imagination that has led me through paralyzing seasons of fear, when what-ifs felt like they controlled my brain. My natural bent, childhood experiences, trauma, and genetics all contribute to the crazy train that in the church world, we call "vain imagination." It's the part of your mind that goes to the worst-case scenario and makes you think no one or nothing is safe.

If this is something you struggle with, these situations will feel familiar:

If you're getting ready for a family vacation, are you making sure the life insurance is paid up, because more than likely, the plane is going down?

If there's a knock on the front door after 10:00 p.m., do you automatically assume trouble?

Do you see an unmarked package in the mail as dangerous?

If you see the school's number on the caller ID, are you already trying to figure out which kid is in trouble?

Those vain imaginations are lies that keep you stuck, and I will talk more in later chapters about my struggle with this. And now I'm going to say something that sounds insensitive, but I hope by now you know I am saying this from a position of love.

Your feelings about whatever you are trying to do in your life, or whatever God is asking you to do, really don't matter.

Since when did your *feelings* become a good reason not to do or try something? Your feelings, my friend, do not release you from your calling.

Even if you feel scared, you still have things to do on this side of heaven. You still need to get out of your head and do what God is asking you to do. Now.

Every single one of us is called *to* things and called *to do* things.

Your God-given calling is your purpose. It's what you are here on this earth to do. It's your life's work. It's the thing that makes you tick and that only *you* can do. It's the thing that trips your trigger because you are prewired for it. Writing this book is part of my calling. It's God's favor in my life which He fully expects me to use to serve His purpose.

And you are called to things too. It's you holding down your corner of this world. It's you taking up the place that only *you* can.

I'm gonna need you to get a deep, deep conviction right now that the calling that is on your life, the thing you keep daydreaming about, the thing you suspect God wants you to do . . . you will not be able to do it if you are going to choose to stay stuck with your fear.

You can't show up for your life, for your calling, for your kids, for your family, or for your faith if you continue to choose to stay tied to bad thinking, bad situations, and feelings that are not true.

It's counterintuitive. Showing up is a blessing. Stuck is a curse. Showing up is motion. Staying stuck is death.

I know these are tough words, but sometimes we need tough words to hit us upside the head and snap us the heck out of our self-sabotaging behavior.

I know so many times in my life, I've been my own problem.

I stayed in places I should not have stayed and did things I should not have done with people who were not good for me, out of fear.

I have used excuses to rationalize why I couldn't or shouldn't do the next right thing or the thing God wouldn't let me ignore.

And maybe you have too.

And that worked for a minute.

But it isn't working now. And it's not God's best for your future.

Your feelings are NOT the boss of you. Fear is NOT the boss of you. Yes, your feelings are real, but they are not in control and they should NOT keep you stuck.

YOUR *feelings* DO NOT RELEASE YOU FROM YOUR *calling*.

We have one more chapter where I want to talk about another thing keeping you stuck, and it's gonna make you want to throw my book and unfollow me on social.

But I love you enough to tell you the truth. And I love you enough to use myself as an example in the next chapter.

It will be a vulnerable time for both of us, but if I can get you free, then it will be sooooooo worth it.

Come on, girl. I love you too much to let you stay here.

chapter eight

IF YOU WOULD JUST LET GO OF THAT

I have so much more for you,
if you would just let go of that.
—GOD TO ME IN MY SUV

A few years ago, I was driving to Target, where all good things come from. But my mind was not focused on good things. It was stuck on a situation that had been causing me heartache for three years.

I was thinking about a friend—well, a former friend. She'd been dear to me for a long time, but for reasons that are unimportant to this book, she needed to walk away from our friendship. I made mistakes, she made mistakes. As two women who loved Jesus, I wish we would have been able to resolve our differences better, but regardless of our efforts, that did not happen. The friendship was over.

And three years later, I was still devastated about it.

As an introvert who puts high value on a few close relationships for the long haul, I don't let many people get close to me.

But when I do, I tend to be in relationship with those people for a long, long time. When I love, I love hard and long. I'm still thick as thieves with my high school BFF, Rachel. And I've been besties with Laura for over twenty years since I loaned her a swimsuit on our first get-together. Once you've shared a swimsuit, you're just kind of in this together for life. #sorrynotsorry.

Losing this woman's friendship was devastating to me. And to make things super complicated because I've always gotta be extra, we were both in a close friend group of families. We lived near each other. We went to church together. Our kids were friends and went to school together.

To say things got awkward is an understatement. We couldn't avoid each other, and our breakup put a lot of stress on all our mutual friendships.

My heartbreak turned to anger, which eventually turned to bitterness, and then turned to what I now know was *torment*. Because I just couldn't let it go.

What I'm about to admit is ridiculously embarrassing, but I'm hoping someone will be able to relate and be set free. Because I was so stuck, I would make an effort to look cute whenever I left the house, just in case I saw her. I wanted to lose a few pounds, because when she saw me, I wanted not only to look cute, but also to look skinny. As if my losing twenty pounds would make her miss me.

And even though I would deny it, I would get upset if our mutual friends hung out with her. These were not my best days, my friend. Nothing I'm proud of.

I would imagine the conversation we'd have if she ever called and said she wanted to be friends again. How would I handle that? I would even imagine something terrible happening to me and me hoping that she would feel bad and sorry when she heard about it. That would teach her, right?

Oh, it's gross, I know, and I probably became a little obsessive.

But when you are knee-deep in bitterness and unforgiveness, you don't think rationally.

Can you relate? I would venture to say that if you're honest about your own catalog of hurts, there's probably a story or two in your life that makes this feel familiar.

And because I was stuck for three years in unforgiveness and bitterness, I can now sniff out someone else who is in the same pit *a mile away.*

I meet so many women who are stuck in some part of their life or business because of a piece of their past that they can't let go. Maybe it was a broken relationship. Maybe it was infidelity or trouble in a marriage that they didn't see coming. Maybe it was a conflict with a parent, or a childhood wound that has not yet healed. Maybe it was being burned by a less-than-honest business deal. We all have a somebody-did-me-wrong song.

And I always find it interesting that people think they can keep their lives nice and tidy over here and keep that dark or painful part separate over there. They think they can compartmentalize their unforgiveness and bitterness. "It happened when I was a kid, so surely how I handle conflict with my boss or husband today has nothing to do with that."

I love you enough to tell you the truth: That just isn't how it works.

You are the same person in your work as you are in your marriage, and in your parenting, and in your friendships, and as a daughter or sister. And you interact in all those relationships based on what you have been through. The health of every relationship you are currently in is dependent on how much you have healed from past relationship wounds.

If you are clinging to things that drag you down in one area, you will see it show up in other areas. If someone feels damaged, hurt, or used at work, they often bring those feelings home with them. A hard day at the office for you or your husband can often mean an uncomfortable evening at home for the whole family. And the same happens in reverse: if there's a mess in someone's personal life, it affects their work (hello, Britney Spears in 2007).

If you have been through something in your personal life that is making unforgiveness and bitterness an issue, don't think that the ramifications of those feelings will not show up somehow and in some way in your work or other relationships, because they will.

The health OF EVERY *relationship* YOU'RE IN IS DEPENDENT ON HOW MUCH YOU'VE *healed from* PAST WOUNDS.

But I didn't understand all that at the time. I didn't realize that my fear of abandonment was causing me to get stuck on this friendship loss. It really had nothing to do with *her* and everything to do with *me*.

So there I was, on my trip to Target, thinking *again* about this lost friendship. And God must have gotten to the point, as all good parents do, when He just finally had enough, because I heard Him speak clearly in my messy, paint-filled SUV that day.

"Jennifer, I have so much for you. But you.just.won't.let.that. go." God was practically clapping in between syllables for emphasis.

I knew right away what He meant. Yes, I *said* that I forgave her, and I would have dropped everything in a heartbeat had she called. But in my refusal to let it go, I had made this incident, this hurt, into almost an idol. I was stuck because I couldn't quit thinking about it.

And now here was God telling me, "Girl, it is well past time to get over this thing, but until you do, I'm holding back everything that I have with your name on it."

That, my friend, got my attention. God zapped me out of a three-year daze in a nanosecond. Thank You, Jesus.

Because I knew that my not getting over that friendship wasn't only affecting me, but my family and friends as well. And I just couldn't let this keep me from God's best for me any longer.

I told the Lord that I was done, right there and then on the highway. I committed to move on emotionally and mentally. And I did.

From then on, every time thoughts of that friendship returned, I would stop and intentionally force myself to think of something else. There were times I would walk around my house repeating, "I forgive her. I forgive her." I began to start praying for her and for God's blessing on her life. I quit letting myself get reeled into conversations that pertained to her, especially when I knew people were baiting me. (News flash: people are trouble starters, and they will remind you of your hurt just to wind you back up again.)

After three years, my heartbreak and torment and grief were finally over. And I wasn't about to pick up that heartbreak ever again.

Now okay, I know that for some of you who are facing huge losses or betrayals, my story may not sound like a big deal. It's not like I had to let go of a husband or a parent. Everyone loses friends, right?

And maybe they do. But the point *isn't* the friend. The point is that I was letting the loss of that friend and the bitterness that grew from that loss trip me up and steal from me. I gave it permission to steal my time. To steal my peace. To steal my attention. To steal from my other friendships. While I was pining over something that I didn't have anymore, I was missing out on so much that I did have. And that day on the way to Target, God showed me I was gonna miss out on a bunch more if I didn't let.it.go. (Thank you, Elsa, for making mainstream what God wants each of us to do.)

Friend, listen to me. Unforgiveness and bitterness will keep you

stuck every time. They are like hands wrapped around your spiritual neck. They will choke the life right out of you and everything
you set your hand to. And they will affect your life, your family,
your relationships, and yes, even your business.

And that's not God's best for you.

I want you to think of a situation in your life that you just
can't get over.

A person that did you wrong.

A boss that treated you terribly.

A bad situation that someone put you in.

Maybe it's been there three years. Maybe it's been there as long
as you can remember. Regardless of how long you've held on to
this, it's got to go. God has so much more for you if you will just
let go of *that*.

I hope that someone reading this has been set free right this
second. You do have a choice. You can move on. The decision is
yours. And really, it does just boil down to d-e-c-i-d-i-n-g.

Well, deciding and obeying.

Let me tell you a story: Last year God asked me to host my
first ever women in business conference. I'll tell you about that
conversation later in the book, but for now, let's say that I had
some doubts. Okay, I really went kicking and screaming through
the whole thing.

One of the hardest parts of conference planning, I learned, was
trying to come up with content. It's one thing to host an event, and
then it's another to take on the responsibility of delivering a message
that is valuable to more than six hundred women from all over
the country who sacrificed time and money and energy to attend.

Oh, and since I'm a follower of Jesus, I knew that my message
would also have to line up with whatever God wanted me to talk
about. So, I asked the Lord what He wanted me to talk about,
and God handed me a humdinger.

For months, I thought about my talks and what would be most beneficial to these women who were coming to the event to learn about how to have better businesses. I could teach them how to get seven-figure incomes. I could teach them how to get more Facebook followers. I could teach them how to set up sexy email sequences. I could give them *strategy*.

But God wasn't having it. And God was making it clear to me that my conference wasn't just about business; He wanted this event to be straight-up church. I was terrified.

I know my audience. They're mostly middle-aged women. A good portion follow me from my painting and DIY days, and a bunch of them are creative small business owners. And yes, many of these women profess to be Christians, but I also have a ton of followers who come with different faiths or no faith. I know they put up with the Jesus in me because they like me and my projects and my business advice, and I love that these women (and maybe you are one of them?) will still follow me despite our differences on faith.

But when it came to the conference, how much God talk would my attendees take? I didn't know, and when God showed me that He wanted me to open the conference with a speech on how unforgiveness and bitterness is sabotaging these business owners, there was weeping and gnashing of teeth from me.

Oh, how I wrestled with God. *For real? You want me to start with that?* Women are here to figure out how they can bring their husbands home from cubicle hell like I did. They want to know how to scale their businesses. They want to know how they can land a segment on TV. They were not coming to talk about unforgiveness and bitterness.

But I knew that I knew that I knew in my knower that God had thrown down the gauntlet, and this was to be my topic. And my job was to be obedient.

And so I walked out into the spotlights that first day of the conference, and I told six hundred women about God talking to me that day on my way to Target. And I shared with them how I have been free from that bitterness and unforgiveness ever since. And not just that; I told them how my life and business exploded after I traded in my hurt and my wounds and my "stuckness" over that lost friendship for God's healing and wholeness.

I shared with them how I had to give up my ideas about being right about how that relationship or relationship breakup should have looked. I had to give up my feelings about the other person, and all the feelings I had about whether I could have handled it better. I had to decide if my future was worth clinging to that story of hurt and loss any longer, or would I do a trade, a holy exchange, with God? Would I trade Him my three-year "she hurt me so bad" story for His better story for me?

WILL YOU GIVE GOD YOUR HURTS IN EXCHANGE FOR HIS BEST *for you?*

I told the conference attendees that I was starting this business conference asking them to do the same holy exchange that God asked me to do. If they had something or someone in their lives that they needed to forgive or let go of, I invited them to write it down and bring it to the front and leave it at the altar.

Now listen, I had no idea how to do this "correctly." You gotta remember that I am not a pastor. I am not a speaker. I talk about big eighties hair and coach women on how to grow their social media lists, for goodness' sake, not how to forgive people.

There was no light show during this session. No emotion-evoking music. No smoke rolling from the stage. Just a group of amazing women having an intimate moment with the God of the universe, who knew that some of their stuff was too heavy to continue to carry.

What happened next was one of the most powerful moments of the conference. I was undone. Woman after woman after woman came to the front and threw crumpled-up papers full of tear-stained words into a not-so-fancy trash can. My team estimated over 80 percent of the room came forward. I saw women set free from things that they had tethered themselves to spiritually for decades. Chains were broken and lives were changed.

Unforgiveness is something that all of us drag around at some point in our lives. It's like that extra ten pounds I'm carrying right now. Even though it's uncomfortable, we get used to it. I can see now that my practical tips about building an email list wouldn't matter if those women were still nursing deep, heavy, unforgiving stories in their minds. No amount of social media strategy can make up for a bitter heart.

If at the end of the weekend, a woman went home to a spouse she hadn't forgiven, or if she was still angry because of that business partner who did her wrong, or if—and this is a big one—she hadn't forgiven herself for making boneheaded decisions that cost her emotionally and financially . . . If a woman was still being affected by *those* things, then nothing else she heard that weekend would matter at all. I couldn't give them strategy and not offer them God's freedom.

Girl, if you're feeling stuck and you have any amount of unforgiveness and bitterness in your heart, nothing I've said in this book will matter either.

I'm gonna tell you what God told me on the way to Target: He has so much for you if you will just let that thing go.

I know some of you are sitting here thinking, "I don't have anyone to forgive. I'm not mad at any specific person. I've forgiven the people in my life who did me wrong." That's great. Thank the

Lord and hallelujah, you are the minority, my friend, and I'm proud of you.

But before you give yourself a pass, look a little deeper. Perhaps you have forgiven, but are you still bitter?

The definition of bitterness is "anger and disappointment at being treated unfairly." Is there anywhere in your life where you feel you were treated unfairly, and it still burns you to think about it? Is there any topic that, when it comes up, gives you that sinking feeling in the pit of your belly? When you see certain things or people on social media, do you feel triggered? Do you roll your eyes and feel a little hot all over at the very mention of their name?

> HE HAS SO MUCH *for you* IF YOU WILL JUST LET THAT THING GO.

I think most of us would say yes, but we don't think that is bitterness. And we certainly don't think of ourselves as bitter people. But here are some ways you can know if you are bitter:

Are you often jealous of the people around you who have what you don't?

Are you easily irritated by happy people who seem to have it all?

Do you criticize or gossip about people when they're not around?

Does it ever seem like a person or a group is out to take things from you?

Is it hard to trust friends and family who try to treat you well?

Do you have trouble giving other people the benefit of the doubt when their words or actions are awkward?

Do you have a difficult time apologizing when you're wrong, or congratulating and praising others when they do well?

Are you pessimistic about good news or new opportunities, always looking for the catch?

That, my friend, is bitterness. And it's smoldering like a camp-fire that you tried to put out the night before, but you wake up to discover is still smoking. Scary!

Bitterness is why you look at social media and wish there was an eye-roll emoji.

Bitterness is why you look at someone and obsess about how they are successful, or thin, or wealthy, or happy, and you aren't.

Bitterness makes you cynical.

Bitterness makes you resent whole groups of people.

Let me give you another example. Back when I owned a decorative painting business, we did a lot of work in huge, gorgeous, *expensive* homes. And at times a few of the women who worked for me would say things about the wealthy homeowners. "It must be nice," they'd grumble. Or, "Easy for them to say stuff like that when they have . . ."

They were bitter toward people with more money than they had. And that bitterness was poisoning them to the very thing that they were hoping to have/be one day.

Truth: You can't resent/be bitter toward wealthy people and simultaneously hope and pray to be wealthy one day. It doesn't work that way. I won't even charge you for that extra tip here, my friend.

Jason and I know someone who has been bitter for as long as we've known him. This person had a super traumatic childhood marked by tragedy, and he became the poster child for bitterness. He is negative in every single conversation. Never a nice thing to say. Never any joy in his life. When we ask about his job, we get complaints. Ask about his kids, we get grumbling. Ask about his wife, we get a cynical answer. You know people like this. We all do. You probably run from them in the grocery store! Conversations with bitter people are no fun.

Now maybe you're thinking, I'm not that bad. I have joy.

I'm fun to be around. But dig deep on this question, because even though it "doesn't seem that bad," bitterness is nothing to mess around with.

I have had to work hard to get rid of all kinds of unforgiveness and bitterness in my life. I only told you one story about someone I needed to forgive, but there are plenty of others. In the words of my friend Hilary, I could tell you stories about my life "that would light your hair on fire." #anotherbook.

I have to check my heart continually. And if you are serious about getting unstuck and doing big things, you'll need to check your heart continually too.

You only have so much head space. No, really. You can only hold so much in your brain, and unforgiveness and bitterness take up too much space. They expand like the frozen bread dough my mom used to thaw out for the Fry Daddy, until there is zero space left in your head and your soul for anything else.

Unforgiveness and bitterness are keeping you stuck. They are holding you back from what God wants to give you.

And, friend? One more thing. This need for forgiveness also means forgiving *yourself*.

You may have done a brilliant job forgiving others who have wronged you, and you're feeling pretty good about yourself. But if we sat down and talked about your life, I wonder if you are clinging to a lot of blame and unforgiveness toward yourself.

Maybe you made some horrible decisions when you were young. You cheated. You left your family. You lied. You were addicted to something and put your family and friends through hell. Whatever it is, where's the line? At what point have you put yourself through enough condemnation? At what point have you punished yourself long enough? When is enough *enough*?

My list of boneheaded, knuckleheaded choices that could have ruined my life or left me dead in a ditch is longer than a CVS pharmacy receipt. And those are long. How I am even alive in my kitchen writing this to you is nothing short of God's grace in my life. And I mean that.

But I am not the sum of the bad decisions I have made. And you aren't either. I am not the same person I was when I made those decisions. And you aren't either. Even if those decisions were yesterday!

If you've asked God to forgive you for the things that hurt Him, others, and yourself, it's already done.

So if God forgives you, and as a Christian your call is to be more like Him, why are you not forgiving yourself?

You've done your penance. Let yourself off the hook. Let go of the pride that makes you believe your mistakes are too big to be forgivable. Now that you know better, you do better. It's time to move on.

I don't know what your "that thing" is, but you do. And you can't take it forward with you anymore. It's affecting your life, your business, your family, and your kids. It's keeping you stuck. It's quicksand for your future. You may not see it now, but you can't cling to old things and expect new fruit.

Forgiveness doesn't mean that anything that happened to you was okay. Letting go of bitterness doesn't make a situation less unfair. But it's over.

What do you need to let go of? Who do you need to forgive? Where can you free up space in order to be able to receive God's very best for you?

I promise you, it's possible to quit thinking about it. It is possible to get past it. It's possible to get back to life as normal. But it will require you to let go of your right to be right.

It'll require you to let go of the hurt. It will require you to let go of the what-ifs of your vain imaginations, because the truth is, what's done is done. Time to pull up the big-girl panties and decide to move past it.

Because you have work to do.

Your kids need a healed mother. My pastor once said, "A root of bitterness is the worst thing you can leave your children." Oh, ouch. That's tweetable.

Your spouse deserves you to be whole. Not obsessed with something that cannot serve you any longer and takes mental attention away from him and your family.

You deserve to get your head space back, so that you can focus on what's important.

God is offering you a holy exchange—your pain for God's plan. So forgive your parents. It's keeping you stuck.

Forgive your ex-husband. It's keeping you stuck.

Forgive that contractor who cheated you. It's keeping you stuck.

Forgive that group of women who were mean to you on social. It's keeping you stuck.

Let go of the bitterness over what you don't have.

Let go of the bitterness over what was taken.

Let go of the bitterness over what isn't fair.

Take your "that thing." Write it down, crumple up that paper, and put it in a trash can. Burn it. Send it away on a carrier pigeon. I don't care what you do with it, but get rid of it. It's the only way for you to be free and get the life that is right-fully yours.

My friend, up till now I hope you felt me hugging you through the pages. I hope you felt seen and vali-dated. I hope you got tears in your eyes because you finally had a revelation of why you behave the way you do.

GOD IS *offering* YOU A HOLY EXCHANGE— YOUR PAIN FOR *God's plan.*

If you don't want to get unstuck, if you don't want to get rid of being overwhelmed, or if you aren't ready to do things afraid, you have my permission to pause here and put down this book until you are ready.

Because we are going knee-deep into that in the next chapter. And this next one may hurt a little. I'll still be hugging you, but in the next chapter I'm gonna start giving you a little butt kicking too. That's because I know that my affirming you won't change your life. Only you getting a holy conviction of why you gotta stand up for your life will.

I'm ridiculously excited, because freedom starts with this next section, sis. Don't leave me now.

part
THREE

ARE YOU READY FOR CHANGE?

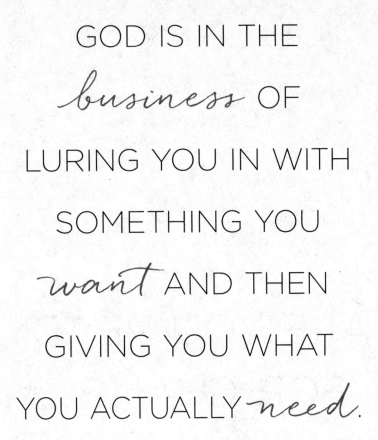

GOD IS IN THE *business* OF LURING YOU IN WITH SOMETHING YOU *want* AND THEN GIVING YOU WHAT YOU ACTUALLY *need*.

chapter nine

RESPONSIBILITY IS NOT A FOUR-LETTER WORD

*A flawed plan executed with ferocity and
certainty is far greater than the perfect plan
executed too late and with timidity.*
—ED MYLETT

As I've been writing this book, I've gotten so sick of seeing my own words. It's a funny thing really. After starting and stopping this so many times, everything begins to look and sound the same. *Blah, blah, blah* is how it reads to me.

And I think it's just because it's been my life for so many months now and I'm ready to land this plane. I'm over seeing my words on a laptop and want to see them in a book.

But there's a hidden blessing in all this "over it" feeling.

Getting fed up with anything is one of the best ways to motivate yourself to change. When my pants are feeling tight and I can no longer tie my shoes without huffing and puffing, I am fed up enough to put down the chocolate chip cookie dough. Can you relate?

And so if you are super sick of being overwhelmed and scared and stuck, well, good news, my friend. That sense of "this has to change," that sense of desperation . . . it's gonna serve you so well.

God can work with desperate. In fact, I think that's where He shines most. I think that's when He most likes to swoop in and save the day. So if you are feeling desperate today, be encouraged.

RAW *desperation* IS A POWERFUL MOTIVATOR FOR *change.*

You've been stuck for long enough. You've been buffering and overwhelmed for so long that you've begun to think it's normal, but it's not. You've fought this same fear for too many years, and friend, it's time to kick that crap to the curb. And I'm gonna tell you how to do it. But it's not going to be a ten-step program or a journaling challenge or a rah-rah session about how you can punch fear in the face.

No, I'm gonna tell you how to get unstuck by using algebra. Sexy, right?

For you math haters, this is easy breezy. I pinkie swear.

In my years of coaching business owners, I've found there's one thing that moves the needle when it comes to getting unstuck and doing the things we are scared to do, and that's determining what's bigger than your fear.

Even though I am the "creative type," I was also a math nerd in middle school. While other kids were out riding bikes and practicing the clarinet, I was participating in math bees. I loved them.

Yes, I know, I am a creative person, and most creatives aren't numbers people. But math just makes sense to me. (Related: I once used pi to help me hand paint a design on a round, barrel-vaulted ceiling, and I've never been so proud of myself in all my painting career.)

So back to algebra. Do you remember the "greater than" sign in math?

$$4 > 2$$
$$175 > 26$$
$$1,777,776,474 > 1$$

And so on.

See, this is easy stuff.

Well, something is allllllways bigger than something. There is always something greater than another thing.

And what I have found is that everyone has something that is of greater importance to them than holding on to their fear.

For example, I may be scared to write this book. What if no one buys the book? What if the book stinks? What if I write it and you all hate me, et cetera? And by the way, fear usually uses big words like "no one" and "you all," because fear *always* exaggerates.

Regardless of my fear of publishing a book, here is my fear (math) equation.

God's call on my life in writing this book > my fear
Setting a good example for my children > my fear
Putting food on the table so we don't starve to
death because I really like to eat (especially tacos
and raw cookie dough) > my fear

Those are my fear equations.

I know that last one is a little dramatic, but it does motivate me to say yes to big, hard, scary things that will potentially result in opportunities or paychecks that will keep the checkbook happy.

So it's super important for you to consider: *What is more important to you than your feelings?*

Because remember, your feelings are a liar. They keep you little and stuck, and you have things to do on this side of heaven that require you to be free.

So what things are most important to you? There are no wrong answers here. No one is judging.

Is finally getting that degree more important to you than the fear of reapplying to a college that didn't accept you?

Is finally having money for your husband to quit his second job so you can be together on the weekends more important to you than the fear of offering your audience a course on how to paint furniture that no one may sign up for?

ASK YOURSELF: WHAT IS MORE IMPORTANT TO ME THAN *my fear?*

Is starting a family more important to you than the pain of trying again to get pregnant when it's already taken so long?

What means something *to you*?

And once you've figured out what's more important to you than the fear and what's more important to you than your feelings, then we can talk about another hot topic: *responsibility*.

Now listen, I know responsibility feels like a dirty word, but it's sooooooo important.

Responsibility is "the duty to make certain that particular things are done" (thanks, Cambridge Dictionary). It's the part of us that is accountable to something or someone beyond ourselves. And so many people don't want to hear about responsibility, because the world right now wants to keep you and me *self-focused*. Responsibility makes us think about people other than ourselves!

Responsibility is easier for those of us who are SRPs because we are preconditioned to do the expected thing, but even so, one of the reasons you are so stuck and living a boringly average life is because you are living like everyone else does. And everyone else is living for self. I'm as guilty as the next guy.

Knowing what you want is an important step to getting unstuck and moving forward despite your fears. But before we can go further, there's something I need to say: your life is not all about you. And according to Mr. Magic, it's also not all about me either.

Ouch, that one hurts a little.

Recently I was "sparring" with Jason. ("Sparring" is what we call passionate discussion, aka "fighting." So in other words, the hubby and I were having it out.) At some point in our discussion, I told him to simmer down, because we were out in public and I felt like everyone was looking at us and I was feeling super vulnerable. And in a way only my husband can say it, Jason said, "Jen, no one is looking at you as much as you think they are. Not everything is about you."

Oh, ouchhhhhhhhh. Way to hit a girl where it hurts. But he was so right.

One of the biggest reasons we get stuck instead of doing the things that will change our lives and the world around us, is because we are living in a world that is centered on *self*. We are so *me* focused (myself included) that we think everything has to do with *us*.

Is that passive aggressive Facebook post that girl just posted directed at me? When my friends don't text back immediately, are they mad at me? When someone asks me to do something, do I instantly start wondering what's in it for me?

Me, me, me. We may have grown up, but a lot of us haven't changed emotionally all that much from our selfish two-year-old selves. We just have a better vocabulary and a bigger pants size now.

But here's a news flash straight from heaven: your life has little to do with you.

One of the things I think we forget about in this selfie-obsessed, can-I-give-you-my-opinion-by-way-of-an-emoji-on-social-media world is that we weren't put on the earth to make ourselves happy.

Your life is supposed to be lived for God and others. It's not supposed to be about you. It's supposed to be about them and Him. And that life is gonna require you to get unstuck.

All over my Pinterest feed are T-shirts and coffee mugs and jewelry that say, "She believed she could, so she did." Ew.

A better version would be, "*God* believed she could, so she did."

It doesn't really matter if I believe I can or not. If God asks me to do something, He believes I can. Therefore, I need to do it out of obedience, because that's all that matters.

News flash: YOUR LIFE IS NOT ONLY ABOUT YOU.

When I started writing this book, I briefly pondered how much I should talk about Jesus here. I had people tell me that if my book was full of God, it wouldn't sell, and if I ever want to see it on a shelf in Target, I couldn't have too much religion in it. (Please help a sister out here and prove them wrong!)

But I also knew that the only thing I could write is my truth. And my truth is, my marriage is healed only because of God. I am alive only because of God. The pain from my childhood has become one of my greatest strengths only because of God. My business has exploded only because of God.

To leave Him out of this book would be impossible.

Now, I know you can pick up books everywhere talking about the universe and all roads leading to the same place. You can find authors dancing around their faith so as not to offend and to make their book marketable to the masses.

You will not find that here. I love you enough to tell you the truth.

Regardless of what you believe, I want you to keep reading.

But at the end of the day, your believing that there is a real God in heaven who created you, loves you, and wants to heal you is the only thing that will change your life. Not my book.

You can keep reading and gloss over all the Jesus stuff, but I am smiling as I write this 'cuz I know how my God works. He has a way of winning people over as He heals their hearts. He's always done this with me.

He has used my story and my life and my talents for years as a gateway drug to have conversations that bring people closer to Him.

I have been hired to paint in people's homes and then somehow ended up praying for those clients. Painting was the gateway drug.

He would place women in my business groups who had walked away from their faith, but because I shared my story in a way that wasn't threatening to them, they would give God a second chance. My group was a gateway drug.

He drew women to my business conference who were non-Christians, and even atheists, and several of them gave their lives to Christ. My business knowledge is often a gateway drug.

Business Lesson 101 is *offer them what they want and then give them what they need*. God is the smartest businessperson there is. He is in the business of luring you in with something *you want* and then giving you *what you actually need*. So whatever you want to do with your life, whatever big, hard, and scary thing you desire . . . rarely is it about what it's about, my friend. God needs you to get healed and get on with it because there are things that need to be done in your life on this side of heaven that have nothing to do with you. #ouch #iknow #hurtsmetoo.

I think this is a book about doing big, hard, and scary things, and it is. But He's not only asking me to write it to get past my own fear; God will also use this book as a gateway drug to lead many of you into a relationship with Him. If that's you, turn to appendix 2 at the back of the book now, sis. I want to talk to you about my God.

And if I never convince you to be curious about this God I speak of, that's okay too. My job is to do what God puts in front of me (write), and His job is to draw people in. I'm glad you're here either way.

But I know that I know that I know that you didn't select this book by accident, and the God of the universe is wildly interested in your life. He has a plan for each of us, and I hope that by continuing to read, you will discover that He has a plan for *you*. Because that eternal perspective changes everything. That's the thing that will get you out of bed in the morning and help you get past your addiction. That's the thing that will make you try again when the first business failed. Understanding why you are here on this earth will help you heal from your traumatic past and look forward to your future. Of this I am certain.

There is something super comforting about knowing someone smarter than me has a plan for my life and that I don't have to figure it out. Instead, I just have to keep saying yes as the plan is presented to me.

There is also something super comforting about knowing that everything happens for a reason, and that God can use it all to bring about good in the world.

And there is also something super convicting about knowing that as much as God loves me and as much as He wants me unstuck and free, that I have some responsibility here too.

A responsibility to Him, to my family, to myself, and to the world.

And I want to take your responsibility one step further, because not only do you have things to do in the world, but *chop, chop* . . . You've got a schedule to keep, sister.

A lot of Christians claim Jeremiah 29:11 as their favorite Bible verse: "'For I know the plans I have for you,' declares the LORD, 'plans to prosper you and not to harm you, plans to give you hope and a future.'"

Walk into a Christian's house, and you'll probably find that verse printed somewhere on a dish towel or T-shirt or coffee mug, if it's not framed on the wall. We tend to plaster feel-good Scripture all over things.

But I've always wondered what it is about this verse that's so appealing. I mean, sure, there's that last part—the optimistic, thumbs-up, God-is-on-your-side, "prosper and not harm, hope and future" part.

But I can't help but see the beginning of that verse too. The first half that makes me sit up a little straighter and take notes. The first part that makes me think that God isn't playing around.

"'For I know the plans I have for you,' *declares* the LORD." *Declaring* feels much bigger than simply *telling*, doesn't it? Paraphrased, it seems like God is saying, "I know how I want this life to shake out for you. I have a *plan*, and I'm declaring it."

So I know God has a plan for me. And God has a plan for you. Got it.

Now here is the important thing I need for you to catch. I don't know about you, but every plan I've ever made has a schedule or time frame to it. Think of your vacation plans or weekend plans or wedding plans. They all have a time component to them, right?

So when God says He has *plans* for us, I also think He has a timeline for those plans. And maybe because I am an SRP, I conclude that God's plans for my life are likely *time sensitive*.

I imagine God with a Franklin day planner in His hands. (Okay, God doesn't really have a calendar, but it's a fun visual.) I like to picture God up there just tapping His designer-covered foot, checking an app on His Apple Watch, and patiently but pointedly waiting on me to get a move on with whatever He asked me to do. I visualize Him saying to me, "Come on, Jen. Time's a wastin'."

I don't think the creator of the universe is time-shaming

anyone if we stall or act slow, but I do think that people act so willy-nilly in this world that sometimes we forget that it *all* belongs to Him. The plan *and* the time.

So before you go tattooing Jeremiah 29:11 on your wrist, remember that not only is God loving, patient, and kind, but He is also God. He has things that need to get done on this earth. And it's in our best interests to get on board, and on time, with His plans. If you stay stuck, things are not getting accomplished on this side of heaven in the time that they may need to. And that delay? That can affect sooooooo many people. *There is a ripple effect.*

Moment of transparency here: The other day I asked our son Noah, age seventeen, to mop the floor. He said he didn't want to because he didn't know how. Now, before you chore-shame Noah, I take full responsibility for his lack of knowledge. If my almost-adult son has never mopped a floor, I have failed as his mother. (In my defense, though, he's been doing his own laundry since he was thirteen, so there's that.)

So Noah was copping an attitude (well, not really, but it sounds better for this book) and making excuses for why he couldn't mop the floor, and I was not having it.

I'm the mom. I want the floor mopped. Surely, I tell him, if you can use YouTube to figure out everything else in your life, then certainly you can use YouTube to learn how to mop. Figure it out and get it done. End of conversation.

After some back and forth between us, I was officially irritated. It's mopping, for goodness' sake. And between us, by then I didn't even really care how great of a job he did on the floor. I just wanted Noah to do it. Yes, it would be nice if he did it with excellence and my floor was spotless enough for me to eat off of, but I was going to be okay with even a crappy job if he just made an attempt. Mopping was now about obedience and not performance.

I waited a short bit, but I realized Noah was still on Snapchat or TikTok or whatever, and my floor was still dirty. Momma was not pleased. We had other things to get done around the house that day, and Noah putting off his chore was (a) taking up my time and energy, and (b) putting other things behind.

And this is where God showed up. In my frustration about Noah not starting what I asked him to do when I asked him to do it, I discovered an inkling of how God must feel about me when I delay what He puts in front of me to do as His daughter.

Oh, snap, did you catch that?

I can't expect immediate obedience from my kids if I'm not willing to *demonstrate* immediate obedience to God.

Well, what does immediate obedience even look like?

Maybe it's saying yes when God prompts me to pay for the lady's groceries right behind us in the checkout line. Maybe it's blessing someone with some Christmas money because we felt led to. Maybe it's digging deep to meet someone's needs when we barely have enough money in the bank to pay our own bills.

If we don't show our kids *immediate* obedience and don't share that experience with them (tell them when it happens), how else will they learn it?

When I ask my kids to do something, I don't want their excuses. I want their yes ma'am. I want them to trust that we are a family, we are #TeamAllwood, and we all have a part to play in this family game. I want them to trust that as their mother, I have a different vantage point than they do. They may not understand why I am asking, but I hope they trust me enough to know that I have my reasons. And I hope they respect me enough to just do it.

And I think God feels the same way about us.

He doesn't want our excuses; He wants our yes, Lord. He wants us to trust that we are #TeamGod and we all have a part to play in this game called life. He wants us to trust that as our Father in heaven, He has a different vantage point than we do.

We may not understand why He is asking us to do certain things, but He hopes we trust Him enough to know that He has His reasons. And He hopes we love Him enough to just do it.

Part of this comes back to the idea of authority. At the end of the day, who has authority in your life? Who are you trusting? Do you really, deep, deep down, believe that the God of the universe has *good* things for you, and that in order for you to fully access those things, you gotta be obedient even if it scares you?

Stuck and scared will not unlock the keys to the kingdom, or to anything for that matter.

I can tell you with absolute certainty that if you don't work to get unstuck and show up for yourself, you will continue to feel frustrated. God has so much He wants to partner with you on, but you gotta be free in order to do that. You owe it to yourself to show up for your life, and you owe it to your creator to show up for the life He gave you.

I know it's tempting to stay stuck, to stay scared, and to stay overwhelmed, but your life is not only about you.

And if you can wrap your head around that and let that idea spur you into getting unstuck, there is so much God can do in you and through you.

I pinkie swear.

Now, it's time to talk about the people you love most.

> I CAN'T EXPECT *immediate* OBEDIENCE FROM MY KIDS IF I'M NOT WILLING TO *demonstrate* IMMEDIATE OBEDIENCE *to God.*

chapter ten

IF NOT MOM, THEN WHO?

Your talk talks and your walk talks,
but your walk talks louder than your talk talks.
—JOHN MAXWELL

A couple of years ago, I was walking through Toronto's airport and minding my own business, when the Lord told me something that He wanted me to share to my audience of creative business owners on Facebook. I could tell that this was from God because the idea came out of nowhere and hit me upside the head, but the idea of talking about what God was asking me to made me feel super antsy, almost nauseous, and scared. That's usually also a telltale sign that it's God—when I want to hide but can't get over the feeling I'm supposed to be seen.

So I went live on Facebook at gate 81 in the Toronto airport, in front of God and everyone, and got the message off of my chest. I shared a story that I had never told anyone before, about something that happened to Jason and me when the boys were little and before Ava was even born.

One Sunday, there was an altar call at our church, and the pastor invited anyone who needed prayer to come up front. That Sunday, Jason and I were bold, and we went and asked for someone to pray with us because times were tough. We were that desperate.

Jason was working a job he hated, and on top of that, he had to travel. With two little boys at home, his travel was really hard on me. Those boys were less than twenty-two months apart, and many a day I was nursing one son while feeding the other Lucky Charms and trying to apply mascara with half a hand. God bless it.

Meanwhile, my painting business was doing well, but because I contracted women to go out in the field and do the actual painting for me while I was home with the boys, I only brought home about half of the income that I billed out.

Our situation paid the bills and allowed me to stay home, but it felt like our finances were constantly being attacked. Every time Jason and I would get ahead a little bit, the furnace would go out or the truck would need to go to the shop. It felt like two steps forward and one step back, over and over. We would make money but couldn't keep it. The whole thing felt a little like filling up the bathtub with the drain open.

We were desperate enough over our situation that we marched up to the front of the church that morning and talked to a gentleman named Mike, both a father in the faith as well as the father of a friend. We told him that money was tight and we needed a financial breakthrough.

Mike asked me to get our checkbook out of my purse, and he began to pray over it. But then he paused his prayer and looked straight at us. Maybe this was it? He was about to declare the financial miracle he saw coming our way? My fingers were crossed!

Nope.

Instead, he said, "The Lord wants to know if you are willing to go to other states."

What the what?!?

I hadn't spent much time before that around anyone who had a prophetic gifting, so the idea that God would say anything to anyone, at any time, was surprising to me.

More than that, though, Mike's question didn't make much sense to me. Jason was already going to Texas for work on occasion. Was that what God was talking about? We lived on the border between Missouri and Kansas. Was God talking about me working more in Kansas? Were we supposed to move? I didn't get it.

I looked at Jason, assuming he would answer, but he said nothing. We just stood there in an awkward silence like a couple of weirdos. Again, Mike asked, "The Lord wants to know if you are willing to go to other states."

Still, Jason said nothing. I was starting to get annoyed, because in my mind this question was for him. At that point in our marriage, I really wanted my husband to lead, and yet I would also not trust his leadership and would take over doing "all the things." God had been working on me to zip my lips and let my husband step up in the areas he was supposed to. I figured this was one of those areas, and Jason was supposed to answer. And yet he said nothing.

Finally, it became obvious Jason wasn't going to respond. He just kept blankly looking at me. And the more he looked at me, the madder I got. Why wasn't he saying anything?

So, impatient, I blurted out, "Yes, we will," and that was that. Mike finished praying over our finances. No million dollars ended up in our bank account overnight, and I forgot all about that experience until thirteen years later in the Toronto airport, when I was coming home from a business group that I belong to.

I was not just in another state but in another *country*. For the last two years, I realized, I had been traveling half a dozen times a year for work to speak or teach or learn or whatever. We were also living in what many would say is a dream home, doing dream jobs, living our dream life.

And it dawned on me: Jason didn't answer the question when Mike asked it, because God was asking *me*.

I was the one who had to answer Mike that day, because I was the one who would be getting on a plane. OMGosh.

It blew my mind.

So right there on Facebook Live, in the Toronto airport, I used my story to call an army of women into action because #GodSaidSo.

God told me to share that many of the women following me were in similar situations to what we were. Like me, they were holding valuable keys to their family's financial future, and it was time to stop thinking and start doing something about it. Even if that meant doing it afraid.

I meet so many women through my coaching programs whose spouses are working second and third jobs. They haven't been on a family vacation in five years, their credit cards are maxed, and the minivan needs new tires. And I am so convinced that many of those women have the knowledge, the skills, and the opportunity to bring financial relief to their families. But they've let fear stop them.

Ladies, we have to do better.

God has anointed His daughters and equipped His girls, and He fully expects His ladies to rise up. He is raising up a group of godly women who are running the race He put before them. God is raising up a group of women who are not just hearers of the Word; they are doers as well (James 1:22). But if we're going to change our future, we gotta quit looking to other people (our spouse, our boss, our coach) to do the job that God has given *us* to do.

Oh girl, I hope you just heard that.

If you are broke, you are a solution.

If you are unhappy, you are a solution.

If you are stuck, you are a solution.

Quit looking at your husband to deliver *both of you*.

Ladies, we are not in competition with the men in our world. (Thank you, Lisa Bevere, for leading the charge on this message.) We girls don't need to run the world. I have zero desire to do that. God is doing a fine job of running it, thank you very much. But we have also got to quit looking for someone else, even our husbands, to fix it all. God has equipped *you*, girlfriend. He has given *you* dreams. He has given *you* ideas. He has given you things that only *you* can do in the world. And you saying yes to those things even if you are scared, even if you feel stuck, is what is going to change your family and change your marriage.

IF WE'RE GOING TO CHANGE *our future* WE GOTTA QUIT LOOKING TO OTHER PEOPLE TO DO THE JOB THAT GOD *has given us*.

Oh, friend. That Facebook Live message is still alive and well on my page because women loved it. I have gotten DM after DM from women saying that is the message that changed their minds.

If this message is speaking to you, go search for my podcast on the topic. You are not weak. You are not a victim. You are not a doormat. And you are not needy.

God has given you gifts.

He's given you talents.

He's given you ideas that only you can do.

And you have a responsibility to Him and to your family to do those things.

One of the most famous women in the Bible is the "wife of

noble character" found in Proverbs 31. Even if you don't spend a lot of time in church, you may have heard of her. But did you know that she was an entrepreneur? She made money in many ways, from planting a vineyard to selling garments to investing in real estate. In fact, the chapter talks about her *working* eleven times. It only talks about her being a mother once, and about her husband a handful of times. This was a woman who worked and who contributed financially to her home. She was savvy and wise, and it blessed her family.

My friend, the wise woman of Proverbs 31 had a lot going on. She was her husband's helper. She contributed. She was doing her part, which allowed her husband to do his part.

Now, this is not me calling for you to drop your baby and go get a job. Don't hear that. I stayed home for over a decade raising our kids, and I was right where I was supposed to be. But I also was partnering with God when He put opportunities in my lap.

If you are in a tight place financially or in a tight place emotionally, or you are stuck and overwhelmed, I am telling you to ask God what *you* could do or should do to help your family.

Your family may need you.

They may need you to start painting furniture in the garage while the baby sleeps.

They may need you to join that network marketing group to sell skin products or makeup or leggings out of your home in order to pay for soccer lessons and new tires.

They may need you to offer your typing or organizing services in order to bring in a little extra money every month.

They may need you to do something to create some emotional and financial breathing room for the entire family.

That day in the Toronto airport, I brought the message God gave me. I told the women who were listening that we cannot defer all our family's financial responsibility and pressure to our husbands, especially when God equipped us with exactly what we need to be a team player.

I don't care that you are scared, I said. Your husband is tired.

I don't care that you don't know how to do it. Google does. Read the help files and find out. I don't care that you aren't sure if your idea will work. No one's sure before they start. God said do it anyway, and your spouse needs you to rise up and do the thing God is asking you to do because it affects him too.

Are you catching that? *Your husband pays for you being stuck.* When you got married, you became one with your husband. So if you're stuck, he's stuck with you!

Ever since Mr. Magic left corporate America to become the CFO of my coaching business, people look at our situation as a dream scenario, and it is. We're both home to get the kids on the bus. Both home to get them off. But I can say with absolute certainty that we are only here today because I did the hard work to get unstuck and do the things God called me to, and because Jason did the hard work of doing the things God has called him to do in this season.

Friend, if you have talents that could help get your family out of the predicament you are in, it's time to stop stalling and start using them.

You have a responsibility to the person you said "I do" to. You have a responsibility to deal with your junk, get past it, and start walking in freedom, because you being stuck affects them too, sis.

And your husband is not the only one that needs you to get unstuck.

If you are a mother (of small kids or adult ones!), you gotta get unstuck for them too.

Our daughter, Ava (#ohAva as she is known on social media), was making brownies last night. I've been working hard at getting my life and my waist right, so I've been trying to get off the sugar train. Do you know how hard this is? (Note to self: the season when you are attempting to write your first book is probably *not* the time to give up sugar. I'm just sayin'.)

So I may or may not have swiped my index finger through the brownie batter last night, because brownie batter gives me life. But then I hear #ohAva say, "I thought you were giving up sugar?"

Who needs to listen for God's voice when you have children, right?

In all seriousness, though. My kids call me out on my hypocrisy and hold me accountable to my goals more than anyone else in my life. They can smell me not walking the walk a million miles away. And in a lot of ways, they are my secret weapon when it comes to doing the big things that scare me.

Setting a good example for my children is *super* important to me. And I want to tell you why it should matter to you too.

(Side note: if you don't have kids of your own, I bet you still have some kids in your world that matter to you. You have neighbor kids, little ones at church, or nieces and nephews that you adore. Or you will have kids one day, so don't glaze over here. This will still mean something to you.)

I am hyperaware of the fact that if Jason and I don't show our kids how to do things despite being scared crapless . . . who will? How can I expect my kids to listen to God's direction, do hard things, and do them afraid when their parents won't even do it?

So much more is caught than taught with kids. If I want my kids to eat healthy, they need to see me eating healthy. If I want them to be kind to others, they need to see me being kind to others. If I want them to be brave, I need to do hard things so that they can see me demonstrating bravery.

When it comes to doing the big, hard, and scary things in life . . . the things that you're scared to do, and the things that you know you're called to do, it's your kids who will know if Mom is stalling and if her talk does not line up with her walk. I think God gives us kids as little walking conviction devices.

Just like Ava knew I was cheating myself out of healthy eating, your kids also know if you are cheating yourself out of opportunities because of fear. I promise you, they can smell it. And if they can't smell it, they can smell your "stuckness" and how you feel overwhelmed, because it seeps out of your pores, my friend. They may never mention it. And they may not even realize what it was until they're older and have the opportunity for adult reflection, but they do sense it.

IF I DON'T MODEL FOR MY KIDS HOW TO *do it scared,* WHO WILL?

When I am trapped like that in my own head, I am not who I want to be as their mom. I'm short, I'm frustrated, I'm distracted. And they know that.

As the mom, the encourager of the home, the head cheerleader for your children, if you are preaching bravery but paralyzed with fear, there is a problem.

If over your family dinner (and by family dinner, I mean Jimmy John's, because #freakyfast) you are telling your kiddos that they should sign up for student council, that they should audition for that part in the play, or that they should go out for the basketball team again even though they were cut last year, and yet you aren't stretching yourself toward the dream in your heart—the desire to run a race or quit a job or start a Bible study or finish a degree—then you, my friend, are not practicing what you preach.

In the words of my pastor, Phillip O'Reilly, "You're preaching the measles but you have the mumps."

And around here we call that hypocrisy.

Now listen, I'm as guilty as the next girl. (Hello, brownie batter.) But when it comes to summoning up some courage and getting out of your comfort zone and doing the things you're called to do, it's so important to remember your children are watching and making mental notes. Your kids will take their cues from you, Mom.

We hire people to teach our kids how to drive, but we never consider who will teach them to be courageous. We count on schools to teach them Spanish, but who is teaching them obedience to God? We teach them how to ride a bike, but we don't teach them how to get our souls out of a stuck place.

Moms, you can't delegate or hire out or pass off to someone else the lesson of doing hard things. This is your job. Tag, you're it.

I believe the degree to which you model courage for your children is the degree to which your kids will walk in it. It's you. Yes, Dad's courage matters too, but I have a strong conviction that courage has Mom's name written all over it.

Now listen, I talk to women allllllll the time who tell me they "can't" start the thing, return to school, get back in shape, take the trip, et cetera, because they have little ones. And I want you to know, I get it. But I often find that moms do one of two things:

1. We use our kids as an excuse.

   Or

2. We prioritize our kids' lives over God's call on our own life.

One thing I feel super passionate about, after talking to thousands of women in thousands of families all over the country, is that our kids have to see us mothers caring about things other than them. We have to stop giving in to the culture that says a mom's life should be all about her children.

Part of the reason this whole getting unstuck thing is hard for women is that we tend to put ourselves last on the list. We have grown so used to putting everyone else's needs above our own, especially if we are wives or mothers. But I want you to remember, friend, that you were someone before you were anyone's wife or mom, and that person still matters.

Those kids *do* grow up. And eventually it *will* be just you and your husband again. And if you have sacrificed everything for your children and made it all about them, who will you be when you are no longer a day-to-day mom, signing homework folders and carpooling them around?

THE DEGREE TO WHICH *you model* COURAGE FOR YOUR CHILDREN IS THE DEGREE TO WHICH YOUR KIDS WILL *walk in it.*

I think moms in America today are in real danger of giving so much of our lives to our kids that we end up raising kids who think everything's about them.

Our kids *cannot* and *should not* grow up to think that everything revolves around them. Because if they do, they are in for a rude awakening when they get out into this world. We are not called to make our kids into idols. God never commanded us to sacrifice all our time, all our energy, and all our money on behalf of our children.

Please don't send me hate mail about this.

Are my kids the absolute joy of my life? Yes.

Do I consider the title of Mom to be one of the greatest honors of my life? Yes.

Will I do nearly anything to be sure my kids are loved and taken care of and all the things? Of course.

But I won't put my kids above the will of God for my life. I can't. And my kids know that. I have told them this.

I won't put my kids above my husband. I shouldn't. And our kids know this as well. Tending to my relationship with their father is the absolute best thing I can do for them. I wish I had grasped this so much earlier as a young, tired, stressed-out mother.

God never COMMANDED US TO SACRIFICE ALL OUR TIME, ENERGY, AND MONEY FOR *our children.*

I believe the right order of priorities for a healthy mom is first God (and whatever He asks me to do) → then husband → then children. But today there are too many mommas who are sacrificing God's will for their lives and putting their marriages at risk because of their kiddos. And this should not be. We have to get the order right.

I talk to woman after woman who tells me she has a dream in her heart, but she will wait to start it "after the kids start kindergarten." Then it's "after the kids go to middle school." Then, "after they graduate." Before you know it, that mom is sixty-five and she's never gotten the courage to do anything for herself, and I guarantee you, that makes her grown kids sad.

If God is asking you to do big, hard, and scary things in addition to raising kids or at the same time as raising kids, take heed. Don't use those babies as an excuse to delay. He is fully capable of taking care of *them* while you take care of *that.*

I was mindlessly scrolling through Instagram awhile back and saw a quote from my friend Jamie Ivey that stopped me in my tracks. "We cannot teach our kids to give their lives away for the gospel when all they see is us giving away our lives for them." I stopped everything and took a screenshot, because #truth.

I gotta do things when God says to. Not when I think it's

time. Not when I'm comfortable, but when God says to. Because the kids are watching.

I can't teach them that they need to do the things in life they feel called to do if they can see I put off God's call on my own life until they are raised.

I can't preach to my kids over dinner that they need to serve the Lord with all their heart if they see me only serving *them* with all my heart.

I can't talk to them about courage and yet not write the book or apply for the job or send the hard email or whatever.

On the flip side, don't read this as a call to put work (paid or volunteer) over your family. In a world telling you that "you can have it all," I would like to offer that yes, you can have it all, but not all at the same time.

Your first ministry is always going to be at home. That doesn't mean only if home is a pleasant place, or only if you like home, or only if home is kind to you and rubs your feet in the evening. No, we are called to home first and to the world next.

Every yes you give to someone or something else means you are saying no to home, so it's imperative that you are not doing what *you* think you should do but rather what *God* says to do. (I'll talk more about how to hear God's voice in chapter 13.)

When I was getting ready to write this book, I had lots of big feelings. I was excited. I was scared. I thought a lot about who would buy it and if it would change their life. And during that time, I heard another social media influencer talking about her book being her "most important life's work."

I was putting away laundry at the time, and I thought, "I wonder if this book will be *my* most important life's work."

And in a nanosecond I heard the Holy Spirit say, "No, these kids are your most important life's work." That humbled me. That re-centered me. That brought me to my knees in repentance.

If I am a success in business, if this book does well, if I inspire women everywhere, none of that will matter to me if I fail as a wife and a mother. And I mean that with everything in me.

When Ava was younger, we would talk about what she wanted to do when she grew up. When she was little, she used to tell me she wanted to work at Chuck E. Cheese, and there was weeping and gnashing of teeth. (Side note: does anyone else hate Chuck E. Cheese as much as I do?) Then she had a phase where she wanted to be a veterinarian.

YES, YOU CAN *have it all*, BUT NOT ALL AT THE SAME TIME.

And then one day she said, "I just want to be a mom when I grow up." And that blessed my socks off. Now, I did tell her to never say "just" a mom, because the title of mom should never have "just" in front of it. But I was so proud of her and so thrilled, because I hoped that it meant she could see the place of honor I had put "mothering" in my life. I hoped that it meant she never felt like mothering was drudgery or unimportant to me. I hoped that it meant she always felt like she had been prioritized over my work.

There is no title, no dollar amount, no position greater in my life than wife and mom. And I pray that my family *feels* that. It's great that I type it, but I often wonder, do they feel that? Do I demonstrate it?

And so I challenge you to look at yourself through the eyes of your kids. What do they see? If asked to describe you, what words would they use? Would they say *my mom is brave*? Would they say *my mom is courageous*? Would they say *my mom is obedient to God*? Would they say *my mom does hard things*? I hope that mine would.

Momma, time for a heart-to-heart.

Are you walking your talk? Or are you making excuses to avoid the things God wants from you? I can tell you with absolute certainty that your kids need to see a model of courage and obedience and follow-through more than they need you to make them another PB and J with the crusts cut off. That'll preach.

I hear people talk about leaving their children an inheritance. And I'm all for that. Leave those kiddos dollars. Make it so, Lord. But I believe you need to leave them a *spiritual* inheritance as well. So Mom, if you have things in life you want to do but are too scared to attempt, I challenge you today to consider: What are you leaving them with?

When God asks us to do something, it's always for His benefit and for our good. It's always to change us and to bring us something of eternal significance. Some rewards we will not get on this side of heaven, but our children get to reap the benefits of our hard yet holy work here on earth.

We all have junk that comes down to us through the family tree. Through generations in our family lineage, Jason and I have been affected by bankruptcy, divorce, alcoholism, abuse, relational struggles, and more. And I'm sure you have similar baggage because every family does! We are all handed things in this lifetime that are our responsibility to overcome and deal with. But early on Jason and I determined that we were not going to pass these same things that we were given on to our kids. We all want our kids to start further ahead than we did, right? Not to need the same counseling, the same therapy? That's our vision.

I strongly believe that the degree to which I model courage and obedience to my children is the degree of freedom that my kids will naturally start with. My ceiling is their floor. Because I am sold out on giving my children a strong foundation, I consider it part of my job to demonstrate action, obedience, and courage even when it's hard. What they do with it? That's between them and God.

It's not that our kids won't have their own battles, because they will. But they won't have the same ones my husband and I have had, of this I am certain. Because we are doing heart work and courage work right now on their behalf. We are working double time to give our kids what we did not get.

If God is asking you to do something, and that thing scares you, step back and consider what it means to your family. Could it be the thing that breaks the generational pattern that you were raised with? If you come from generation after generation of poverty or divorce or abuse, your courage to live a life of radical, courageous obedience even when you are scared is what will allow your kids to experience freedom in the areas where you experienced hardship or pain or lack.

I love you, girl. But what you are up against has little to do with you. You are fighting right now for your children's children, and this is why the enemy is trying so hard to keep you stuck. It's so ridiculously important that you hear from God, get out of your own way, and do what God asks you to do even when it's hard.

If you are a first-generation Christian like Jason and me, you're gonna face additional fun (that's sarcasm for resistance). The stakes are higher so the mountain will feel bigger. In fact, there's a saying for this generational struggle that won't make you feel better but describes it to a tee: If you are the first in your family doing anything, "the first through the window is going to get bloody."

Thank You, Jesus, it doesn't say you'll bleed to death, but you *will* get banged up. Still, the future of your children and your children's children is worth it.

I recently shared on my Facebook page my compassion for the people who are doing things for the first time:

- The first person in your family to go to college.
- The first person in your family to buy a home.
- The first person in your family to be debt free.

- The first person in your family to be a Christian.
- The first person in your family *not* to get divorced.
- The first person in your family to own a business.

I fall into a lot of those categories myself, and I think it's so interesting to me that God reaches out and raises up people who are willing to break generational junk that is on their families. He finds the ones with the crazy stories, tough backgrounds, no credentials—people the world would least expect to do big things on His behalf. Personally, I think it's so He gets all the credit. I mean, left to my own devices, I would have self-destructed. I have no business doing what I'm doing, but God.

But being a first-timer is hard. First-timers get more resistance. Why? Because you're on the edge of changing your entire family trajectory.

If you are a first, my friend, you are breaking patterns. You are rewriting your family's future. *You are laying holy groundwork for generations to come.* And the enemy of your soul is going to do everything possible to stop you.

I believe there's a spiritual side to every battle you fight to achieve what you've been called to do. But what an honor that God picked *you* and thinks *you* are the one who is going to say for your family, "The buck stops here."

I believe if you are a woman who strives to walk with the Lord, you have a real-life spiritual enemy. It isn't your mother-in-law, even if she just threw you under the bus again. It isn't the lady at the financial aid office. Your fight is not against her. It isn't against your husband or your old business partner or anyone else. Your fight is spiritual.

The bottom line is there is good and evil in the physical world, and good and evil in the spiritual world. All we need to remember is that God is for us, and the enemy is against us. It's as simple as that.

The enemy is also not a little red guy with a pitchfork standing on your shoulder and whispering in your ear. No, he is the author of lies who uses people—often well-intentioned people . . . often people we love and who love us—to say and do things that will trip us up.

At the end of the day, the enemy of your soul wants to keep you small. The Bible says, "[He] comes only to steal and kill and destroy" (John 10:10). He wants to steal your peace, your money, and your joy. He wants to kill your dreams and your opportunities. He wants to kill your future, your ideas, whatever he can get his hands on. He wants to destroy your family. Destroy your marriage. Destroy anything he can.

You aren't just fighting the city to get your business opened. It's not just the paperwork that's keeping you from that college degree. That battle is spiritual. The enemy will hate you for what you are doing and what you are changing in your lineage.

The enemy knows that college degree will change you at every level, not because of the paper you receive at the end of all those years of night classes, but because of *who you had to become* to get that piece of paper. And the person who got that paper is now the same woman showing up to parent her kids. And you will do that differently.

> IF YOU CAN'T DO BIG, HARD, *scary things* FOR YOURSELF, CAN YOU DO IT FOR *your kids?*

This is why doing it afraid and hearing from God is so important. It has nothing to do with the triathlon or the course creation or the children's book you want to write. It has everything to do with the spiritual battle of getting unstuck and doing it afraid, and in the process gifting your children with an example of wild obedience.

The great news is, most moms I know will do for their kids what they won't do for themselves. We will make sacrifices and walk through the desert barefoot for days and lift a car off a toddler if necessary. A momma will do hard things for her children before she will do them for herself.

Remember sis, you aren't fighting for yourself. You're fighting this hard for *them*. For your family. You can bless your husband and pass along generational blessings of bravery, courage, and obedience to your kids. You can slay your own dragons so that they won't have to.

You've got this, girl. What's God asking you to do?

chapter eleven

THE WORLD IS WATCHING . . . SO GIVE THEM SOMETHING GOOD TO WATCH

You sow into their life so they can reap a harvest.
The fruit of their life is your reward.
—MARK BATTERSON

I'm online every single day partly because I love it and partly because I teach it. After all, if my job is coaching women how to build businesses in the online space, I probably should be online more than the average bear, right? I'm always trying to stay one step ahead of the algorithm, understand what's working best on each social platform, and that's a full-time job.

But honestly, I'm also online because I feel a deep conviction to use the platform God has given me to teach, inspire, encourage, and motivate others. God's given me a lot of followers, and I don't take that responsibility lightly. I have a deep personal belief that

I am to share my gifts with the world while I am here with this one life opportunity!

But I can remember feeling the same way when I had a fraction of the audience I do today. This thinking that if God gave me the honor of having an audience of *any* size, I had better do right by them. And by Him.

In a similar fashion, I can remember my best friend Rachel telling me that she knew I took my job of parenting very seriously. At that time, my only followers were my children, and they were following me into the bathroom on the daily. Is it not even possible to poop in peace?

But Rachel was right. I do feel like God entrusted these little humans into my hands for just a moment in time. And that one day in heaven, I will answer for how I raised the four gifts He trusted me to raise here on earth.

That feels big to me.

And my audience online, that feels big to me too.

Maybe it's my personality type (hello, fellow Enneagram 3s) or maybe it's evidence of my being an SRP, but making a difference in the lives of others is ridiculously important to me. And for all you young'uns, I can tell you this really ramped up after I turned forty. Something weird happens in a woman when she changes decades, and turning forty was my biggest shift yet. Realizing that I was halfway done with life was sobering.

And I am completely confident that I don't have to change the world, but I am responsible for holding down my corner of it and influencing the people God puts me in front of.

I think God expects *every* gift that He gives us to be stewarded well. As 1 Peter 4:10 says, "Each of you should use whatever gift you have received to serve others, as faithful stewards of God's grace in its various forms."

There is a whole world out there needing God's grace in the

form in which *you* express it. Maybe it isn't writing a book or putting on a conference, but what has God entrusted to *you*? Can you sing? Can you serve? Can you sew? Can you teach? Can you paint? Can you listen? What gifts has He given you that He expects you to use?

"To whom much has been given, much will be required" says Luke 12:48 (NRSV). That means God is saying, "Hey, girl, I've given you all sorts of blessings on this side of heaven, and although I want you to enjoy them for yourself, I also expect you to do something with them for others." #micdrop.

Paraphrased further, I think we could add a PS from God: "So I need you to get unstuck and work through your fear, girl, so your gifts can be a blessing to other people too."

Maybe God has called me to public things that terrify me because the gifts He gave me will help you, a person I've probably never met in person, change your life and your business, and the only way to do that is to put myself out there where you will find me. By watching me in real time do things that I am scared to do, God can convict you to do the things you are scared to do as well.

And to convince you, I have a story, and it involves the rapper Eminem, 'cuz God loves Eminem too. LOL.

A little over a year ago, I went out for a "wog" (this is what I have nicknamed a walk/jog that happens when you're over forty and you still want to be a runner, but your knees hurt).

So I was wogging along, listening to Eminem because he makes me wog faster, when I had a strong feeling that I was supposed to turn off the music and think. So I did.

I thought about how I had just returned from another business conference, and there was so much talk about "manifesting," and people "tapping," and using crystals, and all sorts of things that for me as a Christian had my Spidey senses way up.

Then I thought about another conference I attended recently

where there were seven hundred women ready to make a change in their lives, and I could see they were captivated by the speaker's every word. They were all pumped up for change, and I was so hopeful that the speaker would introduce them to Jesus, because she was open about her Christian faith. But she didn't, and the moment was lost. And those women went home without the ONE THING that would change their lives more than anything else.

And it saddened me deeply because I know in my knower that unless a woman's mind and heart are changed, her business never will change. There are tons of personal development and business conferences giving out great strategy, but also giving credit to "the universe" (not God) and practicing New Age meditation. It's heartbreaking. Not to mention dangerous.

So one day shortly after one of those conferences, I was wogging and thinking, "Gosh, I wish there was a business conference that combined Christian beliefs with business strategy. Because *that* is a conference I would sign up for."

And then I heard that still, small voice: "Tag, girl. You're it."

Listen, I quit wogging right then and there, because on the inside I freaked out. I hate public speaking. This is no secret. I love being part of conversations onstage. I love being on panels onstage. I love being interviewed onstage. But I don't like to speak with a 1995-style slideshow and microphone. Yuck.

But here was God telling me that He wanted me to have a conference.

I remembered my freshman year of college, when I decided to take the required speech class in the first semester of school just to get it out of the way. If I didn't, I knew I would be in the fetal position just thinking about that speech class until I graduated. And that kind of anxiety isn't worth it.

So I took speech class as a freshman and convinced myself that

I would "never ever ever ever ever ever ever never ever have to speak in public again."

Famous last words.

For several years before the wogging conversation, the Lord had been having me speak at different churches and business events, and really stretching me outside my comfort zone. But *hosting* a conference was a whole new type of crazy. And I was not happy about it.

But I made the mistake of telling my project manager and my husband, and suddenly I found myself in meetings pondering questions like, "Well, if we were going to have a conference—I mean, I know we're not, but if we were—what season of the year would we have it in?"

And this is how I basically got tricked into having our first Equipped conference. It's all Jenna and Jason's fault.

In the spring of 2019, three hundred women showed up in Kansas City, and another three hundred women bought virtual tickets to watch online. And I've already told you how it kicked off, with some tough talk about forgiveness and bitterness, and an invitation to come to the altar. Right there at the beginning.

Now I know a ton of women follow me because of my faith. But a lot of women also follow me despite it; they come for projects and business advice, and I knew that there were many of them in the audience that day. I argued with God, and I wrestled around with Him in my soul about how far down the spiritual road He wanted me to go at a business conference. Before that day I had never led anyone to Christ except for my three biological children. Obviously if there's anyone you want to lead to the Lord, it's your kids, but I had never led a prayer of salvation with anyone over the age of six.

But I found myself on the stage of my church giving an altar call at the end of my conference, and at least twelve women raised their hands and gave their lives to Christ. And I believe that all of heaven rejoiced that day for those twelve women. Those are twelve women whose lives have been completely changed for eternity. And that trumps any business strategy they may have come for that weekend.

My point of the story is this. God stretched me sooooo far out of my comfort zone, and eternity was changed forever for those twelve women. And so when I say that you've got to get unstuck, hear the Lord, and walk in obedience to the things God is asking you to do despite your fears, it's because other people's very lives may depend on it.

You may not need to speak to hundreds of people. God's plan for you to change the world may only involve reaching out to a neighbor, a friend, or your sister. I love the saying from Paul Shane Spear: "As one person I cannot change the world, but I can change the world of one person."

God determined your talents while you were still in utero, and I don't believe He chose what would make you uniquely you simply so that you can impress people or earn a ton of money.

No, friend, He gave you gifts so that you can help set people free.

I'll never forget a conversation that God and I had one day while I was in the shower (because all my great conversations with God start in the shower). I was asking God what on earth He was doing with my life. (By the way, I have hard conversations like this regularly with God. He isn't afraid of hard questions.)

To put it mildly, the Allwood family was going through a difficult season. In 2008, Jason lost his job in corporate America right before Christmas, right before bonus time, and there was

> GOD DIDN'T *give you gifts* SIMPLY SO YOU CAN IMPRESS PEOPLE OR EARN LOTS *of money.*

weeping and gnashing of teeth. He decided to start selling real estate, and then ten minutes later, the real estate market crashed in the Great Recession. More weeping and gnashing of teeth.

Meanwhile, we were trying to get pregnant with baby #3, but I'd had two miscarriages, and it was taking forever to get pregnant again.

It was just one of those seasons where we felt like we could not catch a break. Have you been there? Those seasons are painful, my friend.

So I was in the shower, asking God why it felt like He was just dumping everything on us all at once. And then I was smart enough to stop talking and listen to God's answer.

"People need to see you demonstrate grace under fire, Jennifer," He told me. At the time, I wasn't sure how seeing our brokenness could benefit anyone, but I remembered that moment.

I love the verse that promises God will give us "a crown of beauty instead of ashes" (Isaiah 61:3). He will turn things to our good, and He will use the messy parts of our lives to encourage others. If you let Him, and are open with the people in your sphere of influence (which may be the lady at the HomeGoods checkout line or an online audience of thousands), He will use the times you fail and the times you succeed, the struggles and the things you handle with excellence. He will take all your mess and somehow craft a message out of it. I don't know how He does it, but that is why He is God and I am not!

But the enemy wants us all to stay stuck and scared. It's one thing if you let him hold you back, but I need you to wrap your head around the fact that you staying stuck affects more than just you. It even affects more than just your immediate family.

No, your life affects everyone around you. Even your kids' teachers. Even the dressing room attendant at Target. Even those watching you on social media.

God didn't say use your talents only if it's for someone you like. Or only if you are comfortable using them or only if you have a big platform. He said to use them. And the good news for you is that what happens after you use them, well, that is up to God. He completely takes you off the hook. You are commissioned to use the gifts. God will take care of the rest.

But when you're stuck in fear, you can't share your talents with the world or anyone else.

Let me tell you something you may not know about Mr. Magic. My husband is a master in the kitchen. If you have a desire to eat restaurant quality food in the comfort of your own home and gain thirty pounds while doing it (#truestory), we will see you Thursday night at six for dinner at our place. Bring yo' appetites!

In all seriousness, though, my man can cook. He just had his first recipe published in a magazine. I am pushing for a cookbook for him, and it will be called *Making Magic in the Kitchen*. Watch for that. #shamelessplug.

Now if Jason was afraid of what people thought of his cooking, or nervous about the fact that he isn't "formally trained," or worried whether anyone would eat his food, he wouldn't be able to use the gifts God gave him to their fullest.

But because he does, my belly reaps the rewards. Our family and friends are fed regularly. He has cooked for church events and for countless families with loved ones in the hospital or new babies.

I love that he uses his gifts so well to bless people.

I know in Jason's case, everyone is inspired to cook better and eat better when in his presence. Including me!

You gotta get unstuck, girl, because the world needs you.

And lest you begin to think that your gift or your talent or your whatever is not that important, I want to share with you something I often tell the women in my coaching groups. Many of them are creatives. They are makers. They paint, they create, they bake, they sew. And there is a real tendency in those communities to play down their talents.

Creative women tend to "rank" talent. They think being a creative is lower on the totem pole than being a teacher, a dentist, an astronaut . . . you get the idea. They are "just a" creative.

And the truth is, if God had wanted these creatives to be any of those other things, He certainly would have made it so. And what a boring, bland world we would live in without the creatives of the world . . . the singers, the writers, the painters, the flippers, the DIY-ers, the makers, and the passionate ones.

So when I'm coaching a group of creative women, I often need to remind them of the gifts that they add to the world, or at least to the people they know. Because I recognize that for so many women, *creating is saving their lives.* Their God-given gift or talent is keeping them afloat emotionally.

Many of the women who come through my coaching are broken, broke, stuck, or hurting. And using the talents that God gave them *heals* them. It frees them. It makes them more confident to make better choices. It helps them think more clearly. If they learn how to monetize their gifts (as Deuteronomy 8:18 says, "[God] gives you the ability to produce wealth"), then now they have some options because they have some money.

They aren't "just" a creative; they are freakin' rock stars.

I have had women who worked at my painting company who were able to leave terrible marriages because they finally discovered they had a painting talent they could make money from. They were able to finally go on a family vacation or put new tires on the van or put their kids in private school because they used their God-given gifts, put them out into the world (also known as Facebook marketplace and Craigslist), and were able to make money.

And other people see that. Other stuck people see you getting free. And they want that too. It's a domino effect, my friend.

It's one woman being brave, and then another woman seeing it and being brave, and another and another. You have *no idea* the ripple effect of your obedience of getting out of your own way and doing what God is asking you to do.

You have no idea how God may use your story of freedom to entice other women to pursue their own.

I believe so much in this message, and in the importance of getting unstuck so that we can use our influence to change others' lives for the better, partly because so many people have helped *me* change. I'm not just a teacher, my friend. I'm also a student.

> USING THE TALENTS GOD HAS GIVEN YOU *heals you,* FREES YOU, AND MAKES YOU MORE *courageous.*

Through books and conferences and podcasts and classes, I am constantly changing and upleveling who I am and how I think. And some of my best influences have been people I have never met personally and probably never will. I think of Lisa Bevere, for example. Or Steven Furtick. Beth Moore and Bill Johnson. I will probably never meet any of them face-to-face. But what an influence they have had on my life.

And it's not just well-known people. One of my dearest friends is Laura. This woman is someone who knows her Bible inside and out. She is up praying and meditating on the Word of God daily. She uses her gifts every week to pray for people at church who come to the front for prayer during the service.

Her gift always makes me want to be a better prayer. Her gifts stir up my desire to grow my gifts.

Last fall at age forty-eight, my BFF Laura was diagnosed with a bizarre liver cancer that came straight from the pit of hell.

And through the surgery of very skilled doctors, it went right back there. Today she is cancer free and we are rejoicing.

But even when her diagnosis was still brand new and she had no idea what was going to happen or what her prognosis was, Laura was still up front at church, praying for other people who were sick or in need of healing.

Oh, friend, if that doesn't hit you in all the feels, what will? My BFF was using her gifts to heal the sick *when she herself was sick.* What an example to all of us.

You too are blessed in areas that will inspire and encourage the people around you. You've been given grace in the area of organizing or evangelizing or praying or serving. When you post about it on social media or I see it in real life, it makes me curious. It makes me contemplate. It makes me look at my life to see where I have gaps and where I can do better.

Not in a jealous way, but in a "Wow, how do I get some of that?" kind of way. And in a way that ponders how I can learn from you and get some of what you are clearly graced in.

Your gifting can be my blessing.

Your gifting can be sooooooo many people's blessing.

And sometimes people just need to see you slay your own dragons so that they can slay theirs. They need to see you walk through your own battle (Laura up there with cancer and yet praying for others), and see you come out on the other side so they know what is possible.

Please give them something good to watch.

I got an Instagram DM recently from a woman named Theresa, letting me know that she joined my coaching group because she said the Holy Spirit told her to "water ski behind Jennifer's boat and get in her waves." Isn't that beautiful? I have a ripple effect, friend, and so do you. We all do!

Sometimes you are the speedboat and sometimes you are the water skier.

If you're the boat, please remember to act and speak in ways that are worthy of the woman (or a million of them) skiing behind you. Drive well, darling.

And if you can get behind someone who is blazing a trail . . . man, sis, get into that space.

Not long ago, I attended a conference hosted by Sarah Roberts Jakes, the daughter of Bishop T. D. Jakes. It was a sacrifice for me to leave my family for the weekend, but I knew I wanted to go because Sarah had two things I want in my own life: *passion and clarity.* I knew I needed more of both for my future.

Waterskiing for me looked like getting in Sarah's space and soaking in the hard mental and spiritual work she's already done to get where she is. (A pastor's daughter who was pregnant at thirteen? It cost her something to get free!) And I wasn't alone. She had an auditorium of women reaping the benefits of her fight for freedom. Thank You, Lord, for those that battle before us so we don't have to.

Now, not everyone has a boat the size of Sarah Jakes. Not everyone is called to stand on a stage and speak to thousands of women. But there is no such thing as a small calling.

If you are on social media, you are absolutely an influencer. Twenty years ago, if you did something like a marathon or went back to school or started a business, the only people who knew about it were the people in your immediate circle or those that you told on a wall phone with a cord. Well, and the people that your momma or your grandmother told.

But today, someone is always watching you, whether in real life or on the social life.

Every one of us has influence. Whether it's online like myself or with other moms in the carpool line. It may be the teenagers at church, your neighbor across the street, or your brother who's in the middle of a divorce—all these people are touched by your life and your story. You don't have to go viral and have a huge platform in order to be an example.

One of the things that I am constantly telling my coaching students is that we should not despise small beginnings, as it says in Zechariah 4:10. Especially with entrepreneurs, starting small and reaching just a handful of people can be so discouraging.

But it shouldn't be. Everyone starts at the bottom, with zero comments and zero followers. We all have to start somewhere. Jesus started with only twelve followers, for goodness' sake.

God may be moving things in your life to reach just one person. It may be your neighbor or that younger woman at church. It could be your high school BFF or a stranger on the internet. It may be one person, or a hundred, or a thousand. The number doesn't matter. Whoever needs to see your life and your situation as an example, God will bring them to you.

Even if you're not on social media, you still have influence on all those around you. You have neighbors. You have extended family. You have friends and acquaintances. There may be people you talk to every day, or maybe not. Maybe they just watch you live your life. They see you making decisions and doing things, and they can tell that you're fighting for freedom in certain areas of your life, and without you preaching a thing, they are getting a lesson in courage. And.this.is.influence.

St. Francis of Assisi is reported to have famously said, "Preach the gospel at all times. When necessary, use words."

Now listen, I know I need to be careful about making you feel pressured to perform for the applause of people. But really, this isn't about that. Instead, it's a belief that when we said yes to God, we also said yes to however He wants to use us. And He will always use us to encourage others in their struggles and their lives.

When we said yes to God, we gave up our right to demand things look a certain way. The Lord's Prayer says, "Thy kingdom come, thy will be done, on earth as it is in heaven." It makes no mention of, "Thy will be done, but only if I am in agreement, and only if I am comfortable and safe."

And you may or may not see the fruit of your labor on this side of heaven. You may never know how something you said to a stranger affected them to their core. You may never know if your efforts and conversations are actually changing anything. But we don't do it for that. It's not about the applause, and people are not projects.

My friend, your effort and your success is like a breath of air to someone in your influence who is suffocating. Your powering through and doing it afraid is resuscitating someone who is "code blue" in their own life right now.

Will you do the hard things that scare you in order to help get them what they need?

I'm not saying you need a business.

I'm not saying you need to tell people all the things about all your life and all you're going through on social media.

But I am telling you that you do have an audience—even if it's just your neighbor—who needs you to get unstuck and do it afraid and live free so that she has the courage to do the same. She needs you to conquer your own demons and then leave the ladder down for her. She's coming up right behind you.

Give her a good example, friend. The world desperately needs you.

part
FOUR

WHAT'S A
GIRL TO DO?

THE ONLY WAY
TO FIGHT *fear*
IS BY DOING
THE THING THAT
scares YOU.

chapter twelve

WHAT'S FEAR GOT TO DO WITH IT?

*The amateur believes he must first overcome
his fear; then he can do his work. The
professional knows that fear can never be
overcome. He knows there is no such thing as
a fearless warrior or a dread-free artist.*

—STEVEN PRESSFIELD, *THE WAR OF ART*

I was on a phone call a few years ago with a woman I was coaching, and she told me all about how she was scared about something in her business. Honestly, I don't even remember what the situation was, but I do remember that I had on my preachy pants that day, and I spoke truth to her.

She said she felt like she was supposed to do something/try something new in her business, but she was scared, and my answer was, "So? What does your fear have to do with this?"

That left her speechless. Now, I wasn't at all trying to be snarky or a pain in her backside. But I think she had worked with other coaches who coddled her through her fear. Or she'd read the approximately 476,657 articles on overcoming fear or giving women strategies to get past it or punch fear in the face or how to stop living with fear. She gave fear so much power.

But the truth is that fear—hers, mine, or yours—does not matter when it comes to breaking free from stuck and doing the things God needs us to do.

So you're scared? Well, so what?

Now I know that sounds like I am a heartless human being. And nothing is further from the truth. I love you. But I am adamant about helping women see that their FEELINGS of fear do not matter when it comes to doing what needs to be done.

Fear is a feeling. And yes, the feelings can be intense. But you are a grown woman, and grown women do not let feelings control them. Fear is not the boss of you.

My five-year-old, Ari, makes decisions based on her feelings. She falls to the floor, kicks her legs, throws a fit, and cries her heart out because of her big feelings.

We do similar things as grown-ups. We just do it in our minds, so that other people can't see it.

Friend, it's okay to be scared. It's okay to feel it. It's okay to acknowledge your fear is there. God gave you fear in order to keep you safe. You *should* be scared to stand on that cliff. You *should* be scared to look a lion in the face. You *should* have fear when you're on a roller coaster, because they are death traps. (Or is that just me? I can't ride on one without crying and tinkling a little anymore.) Those are rational, life-threatening fears.

Now, what about being scared to apply for a job? Or being scared to go back to school? Or being scared to have a hard conversation with someone in your life? Those are not rational fears. The hiring manager won't kill you. Talking to someone about something that doesn't sit well with you probably won't be life-threatening. Sending an email probably isn't going to do you in.

So be scared. And then move on. So what.

I told the woman I was coaching all of this, and I think she was stunned. And then I told her what I have told thousands of other women. If you *get* this, my job in this book is done.

Ready? Brace yourself.

Your fear does not release you from your calling.

Said another way, it's time to pull up your big-girl panties and do it anyway. We are grown women, and grown women are not controlled by emotions. This is not the sixth grade, and this isn't a dress rehearsal. This is real life and we have got to get a deep conviction that yes, hard things are hard. But fear cannot stop us from doing what we want and are supposed to do.

You're scared. I'm scared. We're all scared. But if you feel God nudging you, encouraging you, wanting you to start the biz, make the call, have the talk, then your fear really isn't even a factor to consider.

YOUR FEAR DOES NOT RELEASE YOU FROM YOUR *calling*.

I know that sounds harsh, and for real, I'm sorry you are scared. Fear sucks. But sis, you've got work to do. You've used your fear as your out long enough. You've given yourself a pass long enough. You are a leader in your home. You are an influence on the people who see you. You are a child of the Most High God. Yep, you're scared, but scared does not matter.

I'm not minimizing how hard this is. Some people legitimately have crippling phobias that they need help getting past. If that's you, I pray that you will seek good counseling and the appropriate medication if necessary and give yourself time.

But most of us are out here using our fears as a way to pass or stall. We tell ourselves that once we beat the fear, we will do the thing.

Friend, the only way to fight fear is by *doing the thing that scares you.*

I'm gonna go out on a limb and assume that if you are reading this book, you have a somewhat middle-class life. You have a roof over your head, food in the kitchen, electricity, and running water. Most of us have a lot more than that.

Can you imagine talking with an HIV-positive widow in Africa and telling her you are scared to run for office, or you're nervous about pitching yourself to a new client, or you are scared to ask that cute guy at church for his number? Can you imagine how women in other parts of the world might wish they had the life that allowed them to have the fears that you and I do?

So much of what we are scared about—I don't want to fail, I'm scared to start, I'm nervous about what people think—are #firstworldproblems. Perspective, sis. Get some perspective. It always helps.

If there is something you are supposed to be doing, fear is not a good excuse to avoid it. Fear will not hold up in the court of Christ. When God asks us to do something or we feel like we should be doing something, fear is such a flimsy argument.

Now I get that fear can paralyze a person, especially people like me who already struggle with a vain imagination.

"I'm scared to start a business, because what if I bankrupt my family?"

"What if I post something on my Facebook page that I really believe but get hate mail?"

(Oh, sis. That's gonna happen. As Dita von Teese says, "You can be the ripest, juiciest peach in the world, and there's still going to be somebody who hates peaches." Dummies on the internet will want to tell you all about how wrong you are. And when it happens, God will be right there helping you put on tougher skin. Because that one voice can't overpower the ninety-nine peach lovers rooting for you!)

Fear shows up in all sorts of weird ways, and with all sorts of weird ideas. I've gotten better at ignoring it, and ignoring my vain imagination, as I get older and realize that a wild, crazy, worst-case scenario voice in my head is not God's best for me. I've done therapy and taken some super-practical steps to help myself not always go to the "we are all going down in flames" place in my mind.

The key, it turns out, is to take each thought and remind myself, "Well, even *if* that happens, it's going to be okay because I have survived every bad situation up until now."

Here's how I learned this. Years ago, I was struggling with suspicion and mistrust, and I was, for no reason whatsoever, worried about my marriage. We had three little kids under six, and I was hormonal and, let's be honest, chubbier than I wanted to be and crankier than I should have been. I was sure I was driving Jason into the arms of a skinny, happy woman with all my crazy.

I would play out all the worst-case scenarios in my mind. What if he left the kids and me for a young twenty-something with perky boobs who had never nursed three babies? She probably wouldn't nag him about things like being home fifteen minutes late because of traffic. His love for her would trump his vows to me, and I would die an old, bitter divorcée. The end.

It was a ridiculous notion, but vain imaginations always are. I was obsessing about it way too often until finally, one day, the Lord said, "Enough."

I was driving down 96th Street in Kansas City in my old SUV, three kiddos in car seats in the back (Lord, have mercy!), thinking, "Mr. Magic is definitely, probably, most certainly cheating on me."

And then I distinctly heard the Lord say in my mind. "Okay, Jen, and what if he is? What's the *worst* thing that could happen?"

Oh my gosh. Really, Lord? I felt all offended. How dare God interrupt me when I was in the middle of my vain imagining? Sometimes we enjoy our ride on the crazy train, right?

But it was God, and so He deserved an answer. "Well, I would divorce him. The Bible says I can divorce him for cheating."

And then I heard the Lord again. "And then if you divorced him, what would be the worst thing that could happen?"

"Well, he'd have to move out of the house because I decorated it and I ain't going anywhere." (I'm still working on my stubbornness.)

"Okay, and then if he moved out, what would be the worst that could happen?"

"We'd have to share the kids, and life would suck."

"And then if that happened, what is the worst that could happen?"

God and I kept going at this in my mind until I got to a place where I realized that if my worst fear was realized, and Jason did cheat on me and did want to leave, while I would certainly struggle and mourn and all the things . . . *I would not die.*

I know that sounds morbid, but God kept drilling down with me until I got to an *aha* moment. I realized I would be absolutely heartbroken if Jason cheated on me. I would be angry and distraught and beside myself. But I would also eventually be okay. God would see to that. And He will see to that with YOU too.

If you suffer from a vain imagination that fills your heart with fear, you are not doomed to your own exhausting thoughts forever. There are plenty of things you can do to manage overactive crazy thinking. (Another strategy is to pay attention to what messages you're taking in. I had to quit watching some TV shows because things like seemingly normal people leading a double life, or running a crack lab out of their basement with their wife and family knowing nothing about it, or living next door to serial killers, will start me on the crazy train, and it's just easier not to get on the train in the first place.)

So if you step out and try to do something that feels big, hard, and scary, even if it fails miserably . . . what is the worst thing that can happen?

If you are thinking about the thing that you feel like you should do, and that God is calling you to do, but you feel stuck because of fear and what-ifs, can you drill it down to the bottom?

If x happens . . . then I will y.

And if y happens . . . then I will z.

And if z happens . . . then it will suck, but I will make it.

See how that works?

This is the truth: even if the very worst thing happens, you will survive. You have survived every awful thing in your life up till now, which makes the

ASK YOURSELF: WHAT IS THE *worst thing* THAT CAN HAPPEN?

statistics of your surviving the next bad thing pretty doggone high.

Living "safe" is a fantasy. But living in God's plan, and knowing the God of the universe is right there with you if ever crap should hit the fan . . . that's the best place to be.

God never told us this would be easy. And He never said your journey would be easy either. He never even said it would be worth it. *He just asked you to do it.*

Now I'm aware that this is a hard pill to swallow. I'm also aware that every book out there talking about fear gives you ten ways to overcome it, five ways to cope with it, three ways to face it, a fourteen-step program of journaling gratefulness to fight it (insert eye roll), and so on and so forth.

I mean, it goes on and on and on. It makes me want to spew green stuff.

Because I love you enough to tell you the truth, and all those lists are fine and dandy. All that may work and help and make you feel better. But if you're spending all that time on your fear, you're giving it way too much credit. You're giving fear way too much attention. You cannot be a whiner when God intended for you to be a warrior.

If you have a heart for God, if you told Him that you were His, if you gave your life to Christ, if you claim Him as your Savior . . . then your fear about whatever He is asking you to do *does not matter*.

Fear is a muscle that you train, and you can train yourself to do things scared. How? By doing things that make you scared over and over and over, and providing yourself with the evidence that you are fully capable of doing hard things.

So you're scared? So what. Take the first step. You're scared again? So what. Just take the next step. And the next and the next, until you string together a life made up of times you did great things regardless of how you felt.

I figured this out when I learned how to swim.

It started on a normal Saturday morning. And I think that's important to know, because often big life and soul changes show up on an average Saturday morning.

My friend Christie had invited me out to a local lake to cheer on her friend who was competing in her first triathlon. I'd never been to a triathlon before, so I had no idea what to expect. I'd run a few 5K races in prior years and was mildly interested in losing the baby weight I still had from then three-year-old Ava. But honestly, I wasn't going to watch the tri. I was just interested in spending girl time with my friend. If you have kids, you know what I'm talking about. Sometimes you just say yes to get out of the messy, monotonous breakfast duty. Can I get an amen?

The triathlon was at a gorgeous lake in Kansas City and the weather was perfect. It was one of those days when I just felt happy to be alive. Perhaps it was being away from the kids for a few hours, or perhaps it was a holy setup.

I was stunned to see that there were over eight hundred women competing in the triathlon that morning. Eight hundred women who got up before dawn to make themselves physically uncomfortable. On purpose. Because they wanted to. I didn't get it. I enjoyed raw chocolate chip cookie dough and binge-watching HGTV way too much to have much practice with the concept of "training."

But as the race began, I was fascinated. I always thought that triathletes had to be in fabulous shape so they wouldn't die in the race and whatnot. But I saw big women, small women, fit women, out-of-shape women, old women, young women, and everything in between.

I saw spunky sixteen-year-old girls racing alongside fierce forty-year-olds. I saw runners and walkers, and plenty of women in between.

But there was one woman I couldn't take my eyes off. I'd guess her to be in her seventies. She was one of the last women to jump in the lake to swim five hundred meters. Yet there she was, in her adorable but non-fashionable, stretched-out swimsuit and her colorful swim cap. She was not obsessing about the size of her thighs or whether or not she had on waterproof mascara, and yet she had my *full* attention. I think she had the attention of everyone around me as well.

We watched her slowly walk into the lake until she could no longer touch the bottom. And then she began to swim . . . with a snorkel. Five hundred meters in a snorkel like the kind I used in the Caribbean when we were on our honeymoon. Clearly, she wasn't young, or fit, or a strong swimmer . . . and yet she swam. And she swam and swam and swam. Not fast. Not correct in form. But it didn't matter.

I had no idea what her story was or what her motivation was, but I thought she was so unbelievably fierce. That woman didn't let age or fitness or the fact that she needed a snorkel stop her. She obviously wasn't in competition with anyone but herself, and that was so beautiful to witness. People cheered wildly for her. It makes me well up with tears to think about it today.

That woman made me wonder if I could do a triathlon too. I was thirty-nine years young, in good health. I worked out sporadically. I was no athlete, but if she could do it at seventy years old, I figured I should, in theory, be able to do the same triathlon the summer I turned forty, right? Perhaps I would get my waist back.

But to participate in a triathlon, there was a gigantic obstacle I had to overcome.

I had to learn how to swim.

Not just learn how to swim *well*, but learn to swim *period*. The truth was, I was terrified of the water. T-E-R-R-I-F-I-E-D.

This is ridiculously embarrassing to admit, but I come from a very long line of "nose pluggers." No one in my family can swim well. I tried to take swimming lessons as a middle schooler, but I ended up thinking I was drowning and had to be rescued by an instructor in front of the entire sixth grade. Just shoot me. So embarrassing.

My fear of water was so intense that I literally choked on water in the shower. Water would hit my face and I would instinctively snort like a weirdo. Who does that? It sounds ridiculous now to even write it. What grown-up chokes in the shower?

But my fear of water was real. Like really *real*.

Still, I felt like I was supposed to do the triathlon. It just kept popping up in my mind. I couldn't shake the thought.

I was terrified, but I couldn't let the idea go, which as I've said, is a sign for me that God is up to something. So I signed up for the next year.

The first thing I did was hire a swim instructor. I explained I needed someone to help me swim five hundred meters and not die. Not dying was high on my priority list.

At my first swim lesson, I stood in our neighborhood pool,

holding my instructor Laura's hands, crying like a toddler. Turns out "bobbing underwater" without plugging your nose can make a grown woman cry.

But my instructor was patient with me, and bobbing underwater eventually turned to blowing bubbles. And bubbles turned into floating. And floating eventually turned into an awkward swimming, and slowly but surely, I learned to swim.

Now listen, I don't want you to think that I turned into a strong swimmer over the course of the year. It was bare bones, y'all. It was ugly. I swam (and still do swim) at a turtle's pace. I could only breathe to one side of my body. I couldn't get my hips high enough to glide through the water, so my swimming looked a lot like dragging a dead body through the water.

Plus, if my stroke got off or if water hit my face unexpectedly, I would panic. Every time.

But by the time the race rolled around—the weekend of my fortieth birthday—I felt like I had done all I could to get ready.

And there was so much that was awesome. I'd convinced several of my girlfriends to do the triathlon with me, because crazy always loves company, right? And I had an entire cheering section. You would have thought I was up for a Grammy. My husband, my kids, my mom, my brother, and my friends all brought signs.

And the race? It was hard and it was ugly, but it was so worth it. And while I would love to tell you I swam like I'd been doing it all my life, the truth is, I was awful.

I had a panic attack a hundred yards in and had to "rest" on a safety kayak until the young, twenty-something male lifeguard, who could swim but had never pushed out three eight-pound babies, felt like I was calm enough to finish the race. I may still be bitter.

I was slow. I was sloppy. I was a hot stinkin' mess, but somehow I finished that dang swim and that dang race. And I did not die.

And something in me was forever changed that day. Not because I finished a triathlon or even because I could swim, but because I did something big, hard, and scary. I did it afraid and it did not kill me. I figured out that day that being scared of something wasn't a good enough reason not to do it. I was scared, but I survived.

I look back now and see how God strung together this entire book out of a journey that started with that triathlon.

I WAS FOREVER *changed* WHEN I DID SOMETHING BIG, HARD, AND SCARY, *and proved* TO MYSELF THAT IT DID *not kill me.*

That triathlon was a holy setup, a training ground for other hard things. God didn't throw me into that to learn about biking, running, or even swimming. That triathlon entered my life to teach me to do things afraid. And then the next one taught me to do it *again* afraid. And the next one and the next one. Of the ten full triathlons that I've done, I've been scared in every single one. I had a panic attack in the water during every single one.

But it trained me. And then when other things started to pop up that I was afraid to do, in my business and in my family, God had already gotten me used to being uncomfortable and convinced me that I could do what I didn't think was possible.

I shifted my business from painting to coaching, afraid.

And I started coaching women, afraid.

And I started speaking on stages, afraid.

And I closed my painting business, afraid.

And we brought my husband home from corporate America, afraid.

And we bought our dream home way before we could afford it, afraid.

And we took in a four-year-old, afraid.

And I hosted a conference, afraid.

That triathlon was evidence *to myself* that I was capable of hard things.

Did you catch that? You gotta convince yourself, you gotta prove to *yourself*, you are capable of hard things.

And the only way you can do that is by having hard evidence that you have done hard things and survived.

Think of all you have been through in your life. Think of all your worst days. You may have felt like you might die on those days, but you are still here.

Think of those nine-pound babies you delivered and those parents you buried and that marriage you fought for and that degree you got after years of night school. Girl, you are strong. You are totally capable of hard things.

So, your fear about what current hard thing you are facing does not excuse you from going for it. It does not release you from your calling.

Fear is not the boss of you.

You are 100 percent, no joke, completely and utterly made for this. Whatever fear you face or past you have or excuse you are using does not matter.

Go, girl, you've got this. Your entire life is waiting for you. In the words of my friend Sandi K., "all of heaven is cheering you on." Don't give your emotions so much control. You are capable of hard things.

chapter thirteen

THE ONLY WAY
YOU WILL KNOW
WHAT TO DO

There is not in the world a kind of life
more sweet and delightful than that of a
continual conversation with God; those only can
comprehend it who practice and experience it.
—BROTHER LAWRENCE

Have I convinced you that you can't let fear be the boss of you? I sure hope so. We need you free, friend. You deserve a life that is unstuck!

If you're convinced you need to do the thing you're scared to do, and if you're ready to get unstuck, the logical question that comes next is, *So what do I actually do?* If you're like me, you're willing to do the thing if you just know what the thing *is*. Am I right?

Maybe you have a feeling you're supposed to start a business, but what is it?

Maybe your heart's desire is to go back to college, but to get what degree?

Perhaps you have an inkling that you are to relocate and you're up for it, but you just aren't certain where to relocate.

Maybe it's just me, but usually my struggle is knowing *what* I am supposed to do. Can you relate?

So this is where I am gonna zig while the world is zagging.

If you don't know what you're supposed to do, you need to pray.

If you have no clue what you want to do, you need to pray.

If you are stuck, scared, or overwhelmed, or have any other issues, you need to pray.

The end. We can stop the chapter right here.

You don't need a crystal ball or a pros-and-cons list.

No need to ask five of your trusted friends and then five more after that because you didn't like their ideas.

No need to meditate or journal or flip a coin.

No "vague-posting" on Facebook to see if you gain any clarity.

No asking people of prayer what they think.

Just ask the Boss.

If you are stuck and if you believe in God, ask Him what to do. Period. Done.

Now I know the idea of praying freaks some of you out because you're not a person who has a relationship with God. This book may have somehow found its way into your hands and you don't know why I keep talking about prayer and God. Girl, I'm glad you're here. You don't need to ask me to pray for your decisions. I don't have a special bat phone into heaven. No one is specialer than anyone else when it comes to hearing from God. I have the exact same line you do! I hope you know I wasn't always a person of faith, and even after I gave my life to the Lord, I was a knucklehead for a good decade plus. I didn't start acting like a person of faith until well into my thirties. And it wasn't until I was in my forties that I really started asking God for d-i-r-e-c-t-i-o-n in my life.

But now that I have, it's changed everything. Everything.

If you have never accepted the Lord as your Savior or are mildly interested in this Christian faith of mine, do not Pass Go and collect $200. Instead, go now to appendix 2 because I want to hang out with you in heaven one day and I want to make this faith thing super easy for you.

> IF YOU
> *are stuck*
> AND IF YOU
> BELIEVE IN
> GOD, ASK HIM
> *what to do.*
> PERIOD. DONE.

Okay, we got that done, great. If even one woman turns to the back of the book and gives her life to the Lord, then the last year and a half of planning this book and my four attempts at writing it, were sooooooo totally worth it.

If you are already a Christian, I want to be sure you still pay attention to this chapter. You probably already know the basics of how God wants you to live because you read your Bible and go to church. You try to keep the Ten Commandments. You aim to love God above all, and your neighbor as yourself. You do unto others as you would have them do unto you, and you (hopefully) demonstrate the fruit of the Spirit: love, joy, peace, patience, kindness, goodness, gentleness, and self-control.

But even if you are already a woman of faith, you are still faced with making decisions and choices where you have no clear guidance from Scripture. And that's where hearing from God comes in.

Perhaps you already hear from God. If so, be ridiculously grateful, because this is *not* common. Many a believer is walking around day after day and has *never* heard from God. Friend, if that is you, if you have never felt like you have heard from heaven, you are missing out on sooooooo much power that is available to you. Your relationship with God is not supposed to be just you sending up prayer requests. That's like putting in an order at the Dunkin' Donuts line and waiting for your bag of carb-laden goodness to show up.

That isn't a *relationship* with Jesus. That's a one-way transaction. Ever had a relationship with someone where you did all the work and all the communicating? Remember how lopsided that felt? Sometimes that is what our relationships with God look like. This chapter will help.

I want you to start looking for God and start expecting Him to show Himself to you. Because hearing from God or recognizing His hand in the circumstances you face will change *everything* in your life. Knowing that He is walking beside you will give you the strength you need, the wisdom to take the next step in His plan, and the confidence you are doing what He wants because He is totally in it.

Figuring out what God wants will save you so much precious time and energy and heartache. It's like having an unfair advantage . . . and He is the secret.

FIGURING OUT WHAT GOD WANTS WILL *save you* PRECIOUS TIME, ENERGY, AND *heartache.*

I see people every day who are hustling so hard to make things happen. They are busting their butts and forgoing their families and striving and pushing and constantly going for more . . . because that's what they have been told they need to do. And half of them have to because they are living paycheck to paycheck and are absolutely stuck.

They need direction.

They don't know their purpose.

They don't feel fulfilled.

They just want to know what they should do.

And although work is necessary and biblical, so many people are working way too hard to get things they aren't even sure they want.

Friend, this is going to exhaust you. The world is selling you a work-hard mentality when what you need is a pray-hard revelation.

It would be so much easier to quit trying so hard to figure out your own life and ask God what He wants you to do. One word from God can change everyyyyyything, my friend. One idea from heaven can do more for you and your life in a hot minute than you can do in a decade.

My friend, lest you think I am a prayer warrior, this is still part of my life that I am trying to grow. My BFF Laura is up daily before her family and before the sun rises, reading her Bible and praying for those she loves. Me? I'm still trying to get a hair wash in twice a week.

> THE WORLD IS SELLING YOU A *work-hard* MENTALITY WHEN WHAT YOU NEED IS A PRAY-HARD *revelation*.

I have a tendency to only get intense and disciplined in my prayer time when life starts to feel out of control and desperate. Otherwise schedules and routines are things I don't do great with. So while I wish I could tell you that my prayer life is consistent and long and intense, the truth is that I'm often throwing prayers up like confetti all throughout the day. I don't have a designated prayer closet like it talks about in the movie *War Room*, because our new five-year-old has moved into the "bonus room" closet in our bedroom. #truestory.

But I make the effort, and I believe it honors the Lord. And I know it has changed my life.

I've been telling you in this book that you do not need to be perfect to start, and so I am going to take my own advice and teach you what I know about prayer even though I am still a work in progress. I'm a shining example of someone who is not where she wants to be, but not where she used to be either.

At our very core, every single one of us wants advice and direction on what's coming next in our life and what we need to do. Each of us would love a crystal ball to answer the questions we have. I think it's why lots of people read their horoscopes every day, or go to psychics, or share memes that say things like, "Something good is going to happen to you today."

But it's not the tarot card readers who have the answers; it's the God of the universe. And He will answer our questions if we ask and then listen for His answer. And there are things that we don't even ask about that God may want us to do, but we must be able to hear and recognize His voice.

We live in a world telling us to write in our journals every day. But how about we also *pray* every day?

We live in a world telling us to set our intentions daily. But how about we ask God what is important to *Him* today?

We live in a world telling us to work toward our life goals every day. But how about we make time to work toward what *God* wants every day?

I don't want you to be intimidated by the idea of praying, because it's not scary. God desires to spend time with you. He desires an intimate relationship with you. He wants a conversation. He couldn't care less if you say things right or use the correct words or have a certain schedule.

But here is where I see people struggle in real ways when it comes to prayer. They ask God to show them what to do. They pray and then pray some more. They keep praying and keep praying, but they *will not shut up* long enough to allow God to answer.

Now, the only reason I can say that so bluntly is because this was me until just a few years back. In my prayer time, I would go through my laundry list of requests. I would lay out everything I was asking and all the things I wanted like a buffet at the Golden Corral. *Lord, would You protect my kids. Bless my marriage. Keep us healthy. Keep us safe. Give my kids good friends. Grow my business. Yada, yada, yada. Thank You, Lord. Amen.* And that was it.

But in my desire to pray over everything and everyone, I failed to get quiet enough to allow Him to speak. I never stopped to find out what He wanted. Sure, I would say things like, "God, show me what You want me to do about xyz," but then I was on to, "And heal Ava Grace's ear infection" before God had a chance to show me anything about xyz situation.

In other words, I never waited for an answer. I never got quiet. I just kept forging ahead to the next thing on my prayer list. I was a bulldozer in my prayer time with God. And this isn't a relationship. If all Jason did was talk to me about what he wanted and continually ask me for things, and I never had a chance to speak or respond, I would be so heartbroken and feel so used.

And I realized, that's exactly what I had done with my relationship with God all my life. I laid out my requests, then went about my day until the next day when I had new requests. I didn't realize I was supposed to be doing anything different.

Somewhere I had learned how to pray, but I had never been taught how to *hear*.

And I know I'm not the only one.

I said this before, but it's important enough that I want to say it again. We live in such a me-centered society. We post on social. We give our opinions on posts. We are so focused on how *we* feel, what *we* want, what's best for *us*, and how we can live *our* very best life every day that it's no wonder we can't differentiate between our own voice and God's voice.

Because we are living *me*-centered lives, we think everything has to do with us. And we get so focused on *self* that we can't decipher between God's voice and our own thoughts. All we've done previously and been taught to do is listen to our own self!

And I need you to know I am just as guilty as the rest of the world here.

Friend, I'm here to tell you that *hearing* God will literally change your life. Hearing from God on what to do next in your life and in your family and in your business is a game changer. It's a secret weapon. This is *your* secret sauce. It trumps any marketing efforts, stroke of luck, or lottery ticket.

Some of you reading this book have been in church your whole life. You were raised in church, and your momma and your grandmother taught you to pray and hear from the Lord. You already have conversations with Him and get direction from Him on the daily. Hallelujah, I am happy for you. Thirteen percent jealous, but happy for you overall.

But that is not my story at all, and I'll bet a bunch of you reading this book aren't sure what "hearing from God" really means either.

I used to think people who said they heard from God were weirdos. Or Bible thumpers. Or lying. But I also had a tiny little part of me that wondered if I could hear from God too. What if it *was* true? What if I *could* hear from Him?

And then, I did.

We had our first baby, Noah, when I was thirty years old, and then twenty-two months later we welcomed our second son, Easton. I always knew that I wanted to stay home and raise our children to whatever degree our finances would allow me, and Jason and I were able to figure out a schedule where I worked six hours outside the home a week and managed my painting business from home the rest of the time.

It worked out really well on paper. The business did well. But the truth was, I was ridiculously lonely. Jason worked long hours, and it just seemed like the dirty diapers never ended. Noah had colic as a baby and just.wouldn't.quit.crying. If you've ever had a baby with colic, you know how desperate that feels. In the words of the great theologian Donkey in *Shrek*, "I'm a donkey on the edge." You know you're in trouble when you look forward to the UPS person delivering packages just to give you a break from *Dora the Explorer*.

I also had no idea what I was doing in terms of parenting. Noah had gone from a cranky, crying baby to a strong-willed two-year-old who challenged me at every turn. There were days when I was ready to lose my ever lovin' mind. Jason usually was home at six o'clock, and I remember some days watching the clock go to 6:05, and then 6:10, and feeling like I was about to lose my crap if he didn't pull in soon. Some days I wanted to give Noah away. (Sorry, Noah, but you gave Momma a run for her money.)

I felt like I was drowning. Mark Zuckerberg was still in grade school at this point, so Facebook was not a thing yet, and I couldn't just go online for support. I was headed for trouble if I didn't get some other women to spend time with, and I figured I needed some Christian women to show me how to raise our kids with decent morals and values since I was not raised in a church home.

One of the things I have always done reasonably well is to ask for help when I need it. I think that is called humility, and I hope I am always wise enough to maintain that position in my heart. So when I hit the end of my rope, I called up the office of the church where we were relatively new members. I basically told the secretary in a way that hopefully didn't sound alarming that I had absolutely no idea how to raise two boys under the age of two, and did she know anyone else at church who perhaps had a young moms' group or knew a little more than I did about parenting than I did or maybe someone who just needed a friend too?

Side note: Some of you are lonely because you aren't desperate enough yet to make an awkward phone call or put an unpolished invite out there to meet new people. Loneliness is often a choice. And in a world where we are more connected than ever before with cell phones and social media and FaceTime, studies also show we are lonelier than ever before. If you are lonely today, I encourage you to make a call, write a text, or send a note to find a friend or a group of them who see you, hear you, and value you. It will change your life.

The secretary was kind enough to give me the name and number of a woman named Becky who had a prayer group every Wednesday morning at her house for a few moms and their children. I called my bestie Laura and told her that she had to come with me, because this Becky chick could possibly be a serial killer and I wasn't going alone (there goes my vain imagination again).

And with our four little kids under the age of four, Laura and I showed up at Becky's house. We ended up praying with a couple of moms every Wednesday for a few years. That moms' group was a life preserver to my soul that at times was sinking.

On one Wednesday in the group, we had on worship music and we were sitting quietly praying and thinking about things. I remember I was thinking about my dad and his health. And I heard words in my mind about his physical healing. The details don't matter (and to be honest, it was so many years ago I can't remember them). But it was definitely God.

I remember being so surprised that I opened my eyes and looked to see if any other moms in the room had heard what I just heard. It was obvious they hadn't. God had spoken to me, and for the first time in my life, I realized it was Him. It was quiet. It was comforting. It was clear.

And in that moment, I felt like I had a little secret that no one else knew about, almost like how I felt when I found out I was pregnant and didn't tell anybody for a few days while I tried to figure out how to surprise Jason with the news. That's how hearing the voice of the Lord feels. It's so precious. It's so sweet. It's so *personal*. And I loved how it made me feel.

Since then, I've talked to a lot of women who have been in church all their lives and have never heard from God. They have followed a list of rules and sat in a pew every week and yet never experienced *a relationship*—a two-way street with the Lord. This should not be so! I am so shocked at how many women love the Lord but have no idea of the power they have available to them. (They remind me of the Christians mentioned in 2 Timothy 3:5, who have "a form of godliness but [deny] its power.")

We have to do better, because hearing from God so that you can partner with Him to get unstuck and do scary things is where all the magic happens.

I want to tell you how you can listen for the sound of God's voice, okay? Because it's only in *Evan Almighty* that God is actually in the room whispering to you in Morgan Freeman's super soothing, soulful voice.

When I am stuck, scared, overwhelmed, or just needing to *hear* from God, I have to get away from the chaos of four kids, two goldendoodles, and my Facebook notifications. For some reason, I like to go on our deck. The birds are chirping, the sun is shining. It just feels right. You need to find a place that feels right.

And I've learned to grab a notebook and a pen, because sometimes God will give me more than a one-liner and I want to remember it.

I tell Jason that I'm going out to pray. And I always tell him I won't be back in until I get an answer to my prayer. I've told the team who works for me the same thing. Hold up until I go ask God.

I start out by thanking God for who He is and what He has already done. I ask Him to remove any distractions.

Then I ask God a question and sit and wait for the answer, just like I would with my husband or my friends.

Now listen, sitting and being quiet isn't natural for me. It requires me to quit the verbal diarrhea and my list of prayer requests. Do you know how hard it is to sit and wait and be quiet in the twenty-first century? When you've got four kids who can feel like fourteen kids some days? When your phone is chiming with social-media notifications and text notifications alllll dayyyyy long? I'm a creative and busy woman with fifty thoughts going through my mind at any given time. The forgotten laundry. The thing I need to add to the grocery list. The fact that I'm a week late on getting a manicure and how can my nails possibly look this janky. What someone posted on Instagram.

To ask the Lord a question and then sit there quietly waiting on an answer requires soooooooo.much. discipline.

But friend, if you can introduce this discipline into your life, *everything* will change. Literally everything. It's like having a GPS, a crystal ball, and a talent manager for your life when you ask God what you're supposed to do next.

> HEARING GOD'S *voice is like* HAVING A GPS, A CRYSTAL BALL, AND A TALENT MANAGER FOR *your life* ALL AT YOUR FINGERTIPS.

God's voice is never loud. It's never shouting. It's never condemning. And once you begin to hear it, you *will* know it. And it's more addicting than any chocolate chip cookie dough that I've ever eaten with a spoon.

I'm about to blow your mind with the simplicity here, but the voice of God to me sometimes sounds like my middle school best friend, Donni Sue. She was the girlfriend I needed to push me out of my comfort zone. She was the extrovert. I was the introvert. She was the one all the boys liked. I was the tagalong in the background. She would have grandiose ideas, and I was the voice of reason.

Donni Sue was also the friend who would convince me to do things that I wanted to do but she knew I was too scared to do. She knew I was a chicken most of the time, but she wouldn't let me stay stuck. She thought I was braver than I really was, so she was often on my case.

She was the one at middle school dances who would stand right next to me and elbow me, whispering that I should ask the boy I had a crush on to dance. "You know you want to. Go." "Come on, girl, you've got this." Oh, I would get so irritated with Donni Sue. I would do my best to ignore her and push her elbow away. Then she would threaten to do it for me if I didn't step up, and so I would always give in and go do whatever she was hounding me to do, both just to get her off my back and because I knew she was always right.

This is how God's voice feels to me. Like Donni Sue elbowing me, trying to get me out of my comfort zone and not be a chicken.

I'm not trying to be sacrilegious and minimize the voice of God by saying He sounds like my friend. But I do think that sometimes people try to make the voice of God into this huge, distant, religious pie-in-the-sky thing, when really, it's the quiet voice in your head that's nudging you toward the thing you want to do but are scared to start.

Now listen, this is how I hear God. But God's voice to you is possibly going to sound very different. The cool thing about the God we serve is that He can't and won't be put into a box. So He will talk to YOU in a way that He knows YOU will best hear. Isn't that a relief?

Whatever the voice of God sounds like for you, my hope is that you will get really good at hearing it, because the next step in getting past your fear is getting good at obeying His voice.

But wait, how do you know if the voice you hear in your mind is yours or God's? This is a great question!

For me, I know I am hearing from God because it will be smarter than anything I could come up with. For real. He will tell me to say something or do something that I would never come up with on my own. That's God.

God's voice will also tell me to do things that I know are right, but I just don't want to do. Take off my headphones and actually talk to the person next to me on the plane. Call my mom even though I don't have time. Return the grocery cart to the cart bin. That's God.

If you are pondering doing something or afraid to do something you can't quit thinking about, those thoughts may be God. If it feels big, hard, and scary but also totally lines up with Scripture, probably God.

Now, let's be clear. God is not a genie in a lamp whom you can demand to speak to, and when He wants to speak to you, He can do it in some creative ways. Your job is not to demand; it's to watch and listen.

Sometimes God speaks to us almost audibly, like at my friend's house. But sometimes it's more like an intense gut feeling. I believe that sometimes He speaks through dreams or visions, or the lyrics of a song, or through a prophetic word from one of His followers. God can even speak through signs and coincidences and angels and out of the mouth of your toddler.

The voice of God will never tell you something that goes against what's in the Bible. So if you think God is telling you to go after that married man at work, sorry, friend. That's your hormones, not God.

And if God is silent? Well, that often means He's still waiting for me to do the last thing He told me. Or He's teaching me to trust that He'll deliver the answer in His own timing, which usually is different than mine. (See the next chapter on that!) Or maybe He's even asking me to open up my blind eyes to see what He's already doing. Or perhaps it's a question that He wants me to decide upon because He is a loving Father and does let us decide plenty.

Does God have an opinion or a direction for every minute of your day? I don't think so. Being told what to do for every single decision in our life is not love; that's called controlling and that's not the God I serve. He created us with freedom of will and thought, and He calls us to make decisions based on those abilities. If a decision is important though, or has the potential to change a life, He'll give us a nudge. But sometimes God doesn't care what I do. I call this living inside God's bumper rails. You know, like the kind they use at the bowling alley for young kids.

When we went bowling when my kids were little, they would throw ball after ball into the gutter. Left to their own devices, my kids were too small and too uncoordinated to bowl right. So we soon discovered the magic of bumpers. With the bumper rails up, their balls could bounce from side to side and still head in the right direction.

I know those bumper rails annoyed my kids sometimes, because they wanted to be big, but they were the bomb for us parents, because they helped us avoid many a meltdown.

And so when I think about the decisions we make every day, I think that God has bumper rails to help us from falling totally off track, and as long as our decisions are inside the lanes, we have plenty of wiggle room to decide what *we* want to do.

We do get to make a lot of our own decisions. Psalm 37:4 tells us that God gives us the desires of our hearts. He loves to bless us, just as we love to give our own kids what they want sometimes just to delight them and see their joy.

So many people are just going through the motions of life without a sense of purpose or direction. But I don't believe we are called to a boring life. I believe we're called to a life of meaning and purpose.

If you're not sure why you're even here on this earth, I encourage you to find a quiet place to turn off your phone and shut this book and start asking God questions about your life and your future. And then brace yourself, sister. Because life's going to be anything but boring after that.

If you're stuck, He has the answers.

If you're overwhelmed, He has the relief for that.

If you're scared, He has the voice of reason that you need.

Ask Him, and then listen and watch for Him.

Everything's different now.

chapter fourteen

GOD HAS
AWFUL TIMING

To us, waiting is wasting.
To God, waiting is working.
—LOUIE GIGLIO

One thing I have learned about walking with God is that He is never late, but He is *never* early either. Truth: rarely is He ever on my timetable.

Having big dreams and plans for your life is important, and getting on board with God's plans for your life is important. But be prepared: the two of those things rarely happen simultaneously.

Over and over in my life I have seen God show up sooooooooo big. But it usually happened years after I thought He should. And during those years, I was often under the impression that I heard God wrong or that His answer to my prayer was no. The truth was, His answer was merely "not yet."

Most of the biggest things God has ever brought our way didn't fit on our calendar. I've termed them *holy interruptions*. They are calendar disruptors.

I've mentioned Ari, our bonus kiddo, a few times now. As I'm writing this, Ari is five. She joined our family over a year ago, and I still feel like Clark Griswold in the movie *Christmas Vacation* when he said, "If I woke up tomorrow with my head sewn to the carpet, I wouldn't be more surprised than I am right now." Ha! We didn't see this one coming.

For ten long years, I'd juggled the challenges of being a stay-at-home mom and also a business owner. I coordinated a staff of contract painters while at the same time practicing ABCs with my kiddos. I changed poopy diapers while I was on the phone with producers from *Extreme Makeover: Home Edition* (we did three houses for them!). I pumped breast milk in the pantry of a new construction project once because I was determined to put my kids over my career, yet do them both, and do them both well.

I have a sense of deep satisfaction that I did what God asked me to do for the time He asked me to do it. I focused on our family, and that is something I will never regret. But after a decade of holding back in my business, as soon as all the kids were in school, I pressed hard on the gas for my biz. And my business *exploded*. Income skyrocketed. My social media went nuts. Doors opened. Opportunities came my way. My team grew. Life was gooooooooooood.

We purchased our dream house in February last year, and in April, Jason quit his job in corporate America. It no longer made sense for him to leave the house every day to go to a stressful job when we didn't need the paycheck, and I needed a CFO here at Team Allwood.

We enjoyed the entire summer together as a family, finishing up our house remodel and enjoying time with all five of us at home.

When the kids went back to school in August, Jason and I had a freedom we had never experienced before. We would get up every day and go work out, then have coffee and read the Bible on the deck. We had lunch out. We got massages. We took Fridays off. It was straight out of that Barry Manilow song "Looks Like We Made It."

Life had suddenly turned a corner, and we loved the new landscape. We had worked so hard for this!

(Side note: Moms, if you are currently parenting littles and cleaning up spit for the hundredth time today, I assure you, change is coming; they will grow up and wipe their own bottoms, and you will have a life again and it will feel glorious.)

Well, we had "glorious" for ten days, and then the phone rang. On the other end was a woman who was a stranger to me, but related to us through a little girl who was my cousin's granddaughter (did you follow that?). We had met this little girl in passing a couple of times when she was a baby, and now her great-grandmother was contacting us to say that Ariana needed a stable home. Could we take her?

Now, here's the funny part to this story. That woman called because she knew that Jason and I had tried for four long years to adopt a child, but it never panned out. She knew we had a heart for kiddos who needed a home.

Adoption had always been something I knew I wanted to do. My best friend Rachel is one of ten adopted kids, and I loved that about her family.

And my poor husband? Thank God, Jason is always up for my crazy.

So back in 2009, we took all the classes and did all the background checks and made all the adoption profile books and checked all the boxes one has to check in order to adopt a newborn from here in the States. And then we waited. And we waited, and we waited.

After two years, we realized birth moms just didn't often select families like ours, with three biological kiddos already in them.

So we decided to adopt from the foster care system. Perhaps a toddler or preschooler would be better for us anyway, we said. After all, we were no longer spring chickens, and we didn't want the new child (preferably a girl) and Ava to be too far apart in age.

There were more background checks and more weekly classes and more paperwork to fill out. Which, by the way, is not convenient when you have three kids at home who need caring for and a busy business. But we did it. We felt called to it. We were up for the challenge.

And we began another season of waiting.

We learned quickly that the foster care system in America is very broken, and very few children ever come up for adoption. Foster care? Yes. Adoption? No.

So after two *more* years of waiting and many close calls, we were exhausted. I was heartbroken. I was sure this was what we were supposed to do. I didn't have a "thus sayeth the Lord moment" with God telling us to do it, but how could He say no to *adoption*, of all things? After all, doesn't James 1:27 call us to care for the widows and the orphans?

On top of my own pain, how could I explain this to my kids? How could we just give up when they too had been waiting for a new sibling for four years now? How could we want to do good in the world and give a child a permanent home, and God just says no?

It made no sense, until another four years later, when the call came about Ari.

We invited this little spitfire over for one, and then a second, playdate. Then we asked her to stay the night "just once" before her first day of preschool.

And then we never took her home.

As I write this, we are in the process of adopting Ariana, our bonus kiddo.

Was this our plan? Heck, no. Jason and I will be approximately

837 years old when she graduates high school. We currently have a senior and a kindergartener, and I am here for all the jokes.

But there's no doubt that this is a holy interruption straight from God Himself. Ari is an answer to our prayer . . . just eight years later than we thought the prayer would be answered.

Honestly, though, taking in a broken little girl when she arrived wasn't at all convenient. My business was booming. We were able to travel like never before. Our kids were all finally wiping their own bottoms and even starting to drive themselves to their events and activities. To tell you the truth, I felt like we had done our time parenting toddlers.

But God had a holy interruption for us, and now we had a daughter who needed appointments and therapy and time and energy and love . . . oh, how she needs consistent, "I'll never leave you" love day in and day out. And adopting a child who has a biological family comes with its own set of challenges. People want to see her. They want updates. They want playdates. So in the middle of book writing and public speaking and TV appearances and so many crazy cool business opportunities, I'm navigating completely foreign territory here at a time when I thought Jason and I were supposed to be "living the good life."

I am not certain if I will ever understand God's timing. But He is God and I am not. It's not lost on me that just when Jason and I were giving up on our adoption dream and dropping out of "the system," Ari was being born into this world. The timing of that blows me away.

Now listen, we adore Ari. Our family wouldn't be the same without her. But our life was full before she arrived, and to the naked eye, there was no time in our calendar for a fourth child.

But God's timing is always the best timing, regardless of what my day planner says.

Speaking of timing, take one look at my Instagram and you

will know I am absolutely obsessed with my boys. I can't imagine not having sons. They are both so handsome and so talented and smell of this heavenly combination of half little boy and half grown man. I still want to eat them up just like I did when they were unruly toddlers. They bring me such deep joy.

But they also drive me nuts. With their ages at fifteen and seventeen, our job as parents is currently to be chauffeur, referee, banker, and event planner for all the things . . . and at this age there are a *lot* of things. Anyone else with me?

> I WILL NEVER *understand* GOD'S TIMING. BUT I HAVE RESOLVED THAT HE IS GOD *and I am not.*

Parties. Get-togethers. Award ceremonies. School functions. Church events. Sports. More sports. More sports. Community service opportunities. Haircuts. Sonic happy hour runs, and so on and so forth.

Throw in a preschooler and a middle schooler, two dogs (one a three-month-old puppy, Lord help us), and a booming business, and the #AllwoodPartyOf6 schedule is hecccccctic.

So it's super important that Jason and I teach our kids the importance of timing.

If you just got home ten minutes late from a night out, don't ask me to go out again tomorrow. That's bad timing.

If you know I just got off a stressful conference call, it's not the time to ask for $20 and a ride to the snow cone place. Bad timing.

Timing is everything.

Part of my struggle in this season is that I can't "stay home" with Ari to the same degree that I did with my other kids. My season is different. My business is different. Right now, I'm raising up a little book baby for you, but that means I'm not playing in the pool with her. I am in a season of traveling to speak. I am in a season of planning and hosting conferences. I can't physically be at home 100 percent of the time the way I used to be.

I've said before that when we started a family, Jason and I agreed that it was important for me to be home with the kids, and I was. What I didn't say was that over time, I developed a sense of arrogance about that. I developed a case of "the stay-at-home mom is the best mom" syndrome. (Gross, I know. Don't send me hate mail; I am still a work in progress.)

I prided myself in "I've never missed a class party" and "I've never missed a field trip." I was committed to my involvement in a monthly prayer group for the teachers and the school. I did all the things.

And I have to tell you, I was not sad when Ava was in her last year of elementary school. I even did an Instagram video about how I couldn't wait for the end of packing elementary school lunches. After having a child in elementary school for thirteen solid years, *freedom was at hand at last*. I had done my time, my friend. I had checked all the boxes.

And then Ari came.

What on earth, Lord?

God and I have done so much wrestling on this. It's been *hard* to go from coffee on the deck every morning to having a human alarm clock demanding Pringles at 6:15 a.m. or else she will run away (#fiveyearoldproblems).

But at the end of the day, I believe with all my heart that God's timing is good.

If I trust Him as Lord, I gotta trust His timing.

And this hard, busy, complicated life right now? It *is* the good life.

Friend, God is never late, but He is definitely never early. And I am convinced after having a new little girl that our destinies will almost always seem like a disturbance.

I wish I could tell you that I am always quick to get on board with God's plan regardless of my feelings, but the truth is, God and I still tangle. I would like to think that I have gotten faster in my obedience, but I'm still often late to catch up. Yet I know that in the words of my smart husband, we're looking for "progress, not perfection" here. So I keep trying.

I don't want to miss out on God's plan for my life because I was busy trying to figure out, argue with, negotiate, or plea bargain my way to a different plan, or a different route to get there. I don't want to miss God's best for me because I liked my timing better than His. I want to be a yes girl. And that includes being more concerned about God's calendar than my own.

OUR DESTINIES WILL ALMOST *always* SEEM LIKE A DISTURBANCE.

And I don't want you to miss out on God's plan for your life because the timing doesn't feel/look/seem right. Just because it logically looks wrong, don't miss it because you are too scared to say yes, or too busy trying to figure out, argue with, negotiate, or plea bargain your way to a different plan.

His timing is always best.

Never early, but always on time. And always worth the wait.

chapter fifteen

HOW TO BE A YES GIRL

Delayed obedience is disobedience.
—RICK WARREN

For those of you who have more than one kiddo, is one of your kids just sooooooo much easier to raise than the others? No? Okay. Then you can skip to the next chapter. (Not really. Just keep reading.)

As I've already mentioned, Noah, our oldest, was a hard baby. Since he was our first, I didn't have much to compare him to. But he had colic. He didn't nurse well. (Who was the liar who said nursing a baby is the most natural thing in the world? #fail.) He was lactose intolerant. He was strong-willed. I was so obsessed with that kid and adored him with every ounce in me. But when Noah was two years old, he kicked me in the shins with his little size 5 sneaker, and I thought I may lose my salvation right there in the Hobby Lobby parking lot.

He was laying the foundation for what was to come. Noah was opinionated and feisty and at two years old could negotiate better than any adult. He was just harder than the average toddler. I remember once when a friend asked me, "How do you know if your child is strong-willed?" And I told her, if you have to ask, he isn't (and all the moms of strong-willed kiddos said amen).

Noah was the poster child of strong-willed.

Then we had Easton.

Now, lest my kids read this and think Easton is the favorite . . . he wasn't. And he isn't. You are all my favorites at different times. I love each of you fiercely and equally. You each have my whole heart. But let's be honest, kids, you all know Easton was/still is the easiest.

Easton was a compliant, obedient kid from day one. He did what we requested without excuses, without grumbling, and without negotiating. He said yes when asked and even offered help before being asked. As a toddler, he would compliment my nail color. As a teen, he would ask me about my biggest struggles in life. He was enjoyable to raise.

Then we had Ava, and we went right back to colic and strong will. I can remember thinking, how can two out of my three kids be this tough? It was like some bad joke except I didn't have the capacity to laugh. It was like the movie *Groundhog Day*, except with kids.

Ava cried and cried and cried. She cried so much that I imagined her crying even when she wasn't. And that little girl was the grumpiest toddler. She couldn't keep up with her brothers, and it ticked her off from day one. Most of my pictures of Ava at a young age are of her frowning, crying, or throwing a tantrum. I kid you not. Come over and I'll show you the photo albums.

Ava was two years old the first time she looked at an outfit that I selected for her, and with her chubby face exclaimed, "I don't like it." She always had an opinion and wasn't afraid to tell it.

Ava had and still has the world by the tail, and I wouldn't have her any other way, but raising kids who are harder is just at times, harder. Why do you think I have so many wrinkles?

And now we're raising Ari, our bonus kiddo, who comes from hard places, and that's naturally going to be hard.

I am assured that three of my children will make great attorneys or world leaders someday, because they sure have the experience with questioning and challenging and bucking the system. But when I really need something done, when I really need some help, when I am up to my eyeballs in things to do and I scan my four kiddos for help, who do you think I ask? Not the opinionated challengers. I ask the easy one.

When I need something done, but I am not in the mood for pushback or negotiation or attitude or a tantrum, who will I go to? The easy one.

When I have a need or have no time or have to make an ask, I go to Easton. I love all four of my kids, but I leapfrog the three who will be hard to get on board.

If I ask for their help, they will want to know why. ("What's Ava doing? Why can't she help?")

They will want to negotiate the terms. ("Instead of doing the entire load of laundry, can I just fold the towels?")

They will do things begrudgingly. (There's grumbling and slumped shoulders, and expressions that make it obvious that if given the choice, they would never do this.)

But the easy one . . . he gives me a quick yes, and that blesses me.

Not only that, but Easton rarely asks for things. So when he wants something, my answer is almost always yes.

Sure, you can go to the movies tonight.

You want a pony? Done.

A new car? What color.

No curfew? Well, maybe not that. But you catch my drift.

Now, Easton is easier but not perfect. Let's establish that. And I still have great hopes that all my kids will someday say yes ma'am at my every request. I'm not letting them off the hook or allowing them to have bad behavior without consequences or discipline.

But as a parent, it's just such a *huge* blessing when our kids do what we ask. An easy yes is such a gift.

And I wonder if God feels the same way about us. I wonder if when He needs something done, does He leapfrog the doubting, challenging, negotiating people and just ask the ones who will give Him an easy yes? When I get to heaven, I'm going to ask. (Along with why are there hot flashes and mosquitos, God? What was the point of *that*?)

Man, I want to be an easy child for God. I want to be that breath of fresh air that just gets on board quickly and with a good attitude.

I want to have a reputation in heaven of being a yes girl. I want to be known as someone God can count on to do things on His behalf. I want Him to remember *me*. I want Him to remember me as His daughter who will do His work willingly, without attitude, and when He asks.

> *I want to be* A YES GIRL FOR GOD. I WANT A REPUTATION *in heaven* FOR BEING SOMEONE HE CAN COUNT ON.

Now listen, before you send me hate mail, I know in God's perfection He doesn't parent like I do. But in 2 Chronicles 16:9, He tells us that "the eyes of the Lord range throughout the earth to strengthen those whose hearts are fully committed to him." Almost like He is scanning His kids to see who He can ask and who He can depend on for an easy yes. The same thing I do as a mother.

Being God's yes girl, though, means saying yes regardless of my feelings. Regardless of my fear. Regardless of my knowledge or my confidence or my thoughts on His ask or whatever. And regardless of my current calendar space.

My job on this side of heaven, not to mention my responsibility in other people's lives, depends on my obedience, no matter what I'm feeling.

And so does yours.

You might have picked up this book to find out how to get over the stuff that's holding you back so you can live the life you want, but I have to tell you: the way to get the life you're meant to live is not by just doing whatever you want. If you've given God the highest place in your life, then you don't get to pick how God uses you.

Have you seen the meme floating around the internet that says, "Good things come to those who hustle"?

This is so much truer: *Good things come to those who are obedient.*

Hustling may or may not result in much. I coach women every day who have been hustling for decades. Hustling for so long that their body is betraying them and their families resent them.

Hustling is never the answer to any problem. Saying yes and being obedient are.

Another one of those memes I see a lot says, "Do more of what makes you feel good."

Uh, no. If I do more of what makes me feel good, I will spend my day eating raw chocolate chip cookie dough and surfing Pinterest.

The truth is: *Do more of what God tells you to do.*

People also say, "Everything you want is on the other side of fear." No, it isn't.

Everything you want is on the other side of your obedience.

Whatever happened to doing things we are supposed to do simply because we are supposed to? Like saying yes to your parents. Staying married even when it's hard. Staying in friendships that are challenging but grow you. Staying in church even though the worship is a little too loud or you don't like the new service times.

Nike did not have it wrong, my friend. As long as "it" is what God told you to do, then you need to just do it.

If you're sensing God asking you to do something or you are feeling a "holy nudge," I hope you will do it. I hope you will not try to rationalize, bargain, or argue your way out of it, because He is your Father. He knows best. He is for you and not against you.

GOOD THINGS COME TO THOSE WHO ARE *obedient.*

And while He is crazy about you and obsessed with you, I also don't think God cares about the excuses you have. Your reasons why you "can't" don't really matter if He asked you to do something.

No, you are not too old.

No, you are not too young.

Yes, you know enough.

No, you don't need more time.

No, there is not a perfect time.

Yes, you are capable.

No, you don't need another sign.

Yes, you can.

And the list goes on and on.

God is God, my friend. And like a strong-willed toddler, He wants what He wants. But unlike a toddler, He deserves to get what He wants.

He doesn't care if it's inconvenient or an intrusion or bad timing.

It doesn't matter if you are uncomfortable, or not, in your opinion, the most capable.

It's okay that you don't know everything. Clearly you know enough, or God wouldn't ask.

Your job is just to say yes.

I look at my relationship with God most often as a father-daughter relationship.

Now, I was raised in a household where obedience was of utmost value. In the seventies, parenting was much different than it is today. Some of you will remember this. We weren't given an opportunity for debate or argument. When my dad told us kids to do something, that was it. I may not like it, but I did it.

Today, I'm convicted by the question, *Do I have that same level of respect and reverence for my heavenly Father?* When I suspect He has a plan for me, when I suspect He is asking something of me, is it a done deal, or do I consider it up for debate? Do I instinctively say yes without wondering how it will all work out? And do I say yes immediately, or do I stall and dillydally under the guise of "waiting for confirmation," even though I know full good and well what God just asked of me?

Because remember what we talked about before? My heavenly Daddy has a plan and a timeline, and it's my job to get on board with it. And so I'm convinced of this:

Delayed obedience is disobedience.

Stop and read that again, sis.

Is the opportunity gone if I move too slow? Like, will God go on to the next person if I continue to stall, fight, and put off what He asks me to do? I'm not sure there is theology to support it, but how often do you have an idea and not do anything with it, only to see someone else doing it? Oh, this hit me the other day when I saw someone announce a product that was so similar to one God's been nudging me to design, but I put it off because I "didn't know where to start." (Sound familiar?) The public figure launching the product doesn't know me. She doesn't know how God put this idea in my head three years ago. And in my gut, I wonder if God finally gave her the same idea because He knew she would say yes.

Ouch. That idea both hurts and scares me, friend, and it should give you a holy scare too.

The good news is, God is a super-patient-and-always-rooting-for-us kind of dad. So I do think that even when we are knuckle-heads, He is ever loving and ridiculously patient, and when it comes to God's plans for your life, getting on board late is probably better than getting on board never.

But at the end of the day, He wants our yes, and He wants it *now*.

Our current calendar or capacity or knowledge level isn't what defines what we're capable of.

The longer we delay in saying yes and amen, the longer we are outside of God's best for us.

Can you and I be an easy yes for God? Can we have a repu-tation in heaven for being a yes girl?

Well, that starts with our saying yes. I'm in if you are.

Let's take the first step in the next chapter.

chapter sixteen

TAKE THE FIRST STEP

> *Everyone who's ever taken a shower*
> *has had an idea. It's the person who gets out*
> *of the shower, dries off, and does something*
> *about it who makes a difference.*
> **—NOLAN BUSHNELL, CREATOR OF**
> **THE ATARI VIDEO GAME SYSTEM**

My husband is making me take hip-hop dance lessons.

Sigh

Well, he's not really making me. He's just giving me the full-court press, but only because I have been talking about hip-hop classes for about three years without doing anything about it. And I made him a bet the other day (when will I learn that I lose all bets?), and so here we are.

See, back in the day of Aussie grape-scented hairspray and rolling our jeans at the ankle, I danced on the drill team in my hometown of Moville, Iowa. It was one of my absolute favorite things to do. Even though I was a complete introvert, I loved being on the dance floor with a bunch of girls doing routines to songs like "Queen of Hearts." I wish you could have seen us with our big blonde bangs and baggy skirts, doing what we thought were "bold moves." We were hot stuff. Those were the days.

I loved going to dance clubs as a teenager and then danced my way through my wild early twenties. Then I got my life together, and I quit going places where dancing was even happening.

For years, certain genres of music (the kind I liked to dance to) were very triggering for me. They reminded me of a time when I was not my best self and making poor decisions. So I quit even listening to the type of music that really made me want to dance. And then I quit dancing altogether, because I got hyperaware of myself, my moves, my age, my stiffness. I had all the excuses.

Today, enough years have passed, and I've grown up enough and healed enough that I've been able to go back to listening to the hip-hop dance music that I still adore. And it makes me want to dance again.

But do you know what happens when a woman who hasn't danced in thirty-plus years tries to dance? It's awkward. It's rusty. It's not fun to watch, and it's not fun to do, because *why don't I look in the mirror like I look in my mind?* Ugghh, I am mortified by my middle-aged-ness.

And so, I've been resisting taking a hip-hop class for years now, because more than likely, I will be the oldest person in the class. I've been resisting, because more than likely, I will be the least talented dancer there. I've been resisting, because I am certain I'm going to feel foolish and old and uncoordinated and embarrassed, and none of those are feelings that I willingly embrace. Plus, the older I get, the more introverted I become. Now, the idea of dancing in front of anyone without a margarita in me makes me feel exceptionally exposed and vulnerable. Can you relate?

But the hip-hop dance class idea just wouldn't give up on me. I kept bumping into it wherever I turned. I saw other people on social media who were taking hip-hop dance classes. I even had a dream that I danced onstage with another business coach at a conference.

And it irritates the heck out of me when things like this happen. When I keep bumping up against an idea again and again and again. Especially if it's an idea that I've been avoiding. I'm sure this happens to you too—you get a thought that just won't let you forget it, like a paper cut on your finger that you keep bumping or a fly in your car that keeps bouncing and buzzing against the windows.

Whenever this happens, I know God is up to something. He isn't speaking this to you in prayer time. It isn't something you even know God is orchestrating on your behalf. It just seems like a thing that keeps popping up, an idea, a hunch, a what-if. Oh, friend, God is up to something every stinkin' time. Trust me on this.

WHEN I CAN'T *get away* FROM AN IDEA, I KNOW GOD IS UP TO *something*.

And you may never know what it is, and maybe it's just for joy. But I love when I can't get away from something. Because I know God is up to something.

And when I sense God is up to something, it's best that I pay attention and link arms. So, I googled hip-hop dance classes near me. I looked for personal coaches who would come to my house. I researched online hip-hop classes. And finally, right before I sat down to write this chapter, I signed up for a class at a local studio.

I may die of humiliation. Or being out of shape. Or everyone looking at the new girl who is old and fluffy. But girl, I don't even care, because I've learned if I can't get away from an idea, I do my best to chase it. This is how my business has made millions of dollars. This is why I am writing a book. This is why I've done ten triathlons.

But what so often happens when we feel like God is nudging us to do something is that we get hung up before we even start.

Because the idea doesn't make sense.

It feels foolish.

We get discouraged because we try to look all the way down the lane to the finish line, and it seems so.far.away. And it very well could be.

Maybe you want to run a half marathon, but you haven't worked out in years.

Maybe you want a successful jewelry business, but there are already nine million of them on the internet and you think it will take you half a century to become Kendra Scott.

Maybe you're jogging to your favorite Eminem song on a random Sunday afternoon, and your imagination is filled with the idea of hosting your own conference, which is such a huge endeavor and makes you want to cry with frustration. . . . Oh wait, that was me.

Girl, I get it. Anytime we begin something new, we have no idea how long it will take. Or if it will work. Essentially, we're rolling the dice, because we can't see what's down the road.

But I have some big thoughts here that will help get you unstuck so you can *start*. Because getting stuck usually happens in the beginning when we're scared to start something new.

Beginnings are hard. They're scary. But the beginning is also when new momentum is established.

If you begin that business, your family may be set free financially.

If you begin going to church, your family may be set free spiritually.

If you begin to go back to school, you may find you love the educational system and want to be a teacher. Then you'll have the ability to positively affect hundreds or thousands of children in your career.

Whatever your thing is, starting it could create a spiritual wildfire that changes the lives of everyone around you.

But that's all in the future, and the fear is all in the *now*. And we're used to focusing on the *now*.

If I pull up Netflix tonight, I have my choice of about 1,376,223 shows.

My kids want mac and cheese in the microwave *now*, and we all want Amazon Prime at our front door tomorrow.

When we remodeled our house, Jason and I planted *mature* trees in our landscaping because I didn't want to buy small ones and then wait years for them to grow.

I made every member of my family get TSA PreCheck so we don't have to wait in airport lines. And I want the special passes at amusement parks that get us to the front of the lines. Because lines steal my soul.

Sound familiar? I'm sure I'm not the only one who doesn't want to wait for anything. We live in a world that trains us to expect everything immediately. But starting something new and something of any depth doesn't get accomplished overnight. Doing something new generally means we forfeit the chance to see a huge result *now*.

I guarantee I won't be a great hip-hop dancer after my first lesson. And the truth is, I probably never will be.

But I want to ask you. Will your seed of a dream ever grow to the fullness that you imagine?

Friend, it's best you don't know.

Most of us think we want to know how everything in our lives will work out. We want to know where we will end up. But what I've learned is that we should rethink that. Ignorance really *is* bliss.

Author and pastor Joel Osteen says, "If God showed you what He has in store, where He's taking you, it would not only excite you, you would not only be amazed, but when you saw what it's going to take to get you there—the giants you're going to have to face, the lonely nights, the betrayals, the closed doors, the Pharaohs you're going to have to stand before—you would think 'No thanks, God. I'll just stay where I am.'"*

I believe with my whole heart that it's because of God's goodness that He doesn't show us the whole picture or give us the whole plan in advance, because I bet it would intimidate the heck out of us.

Honey, I promise you . . . it's better we don't know.

If God had shown me nineteen years ago when I started my precious little painting company where my life would be today, coaching thousands of women every month, I would have been in a corner sucking my thumb. I never could have handled it.

I bet you know someone who got a promotion, got some money, got elevated in some way, but then couldn't handle it. Look at lottery winners. Did you know 80 percent of lottery winners go bankrupt in five years? They aren't ready for that kind of gift. They can't handle the pressure.

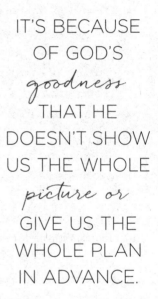

IT'S BECAUSE OF GOD'S *goodness* THAT HE DOESN'T SHOW US THE WHOLE *picture or* GIVE US THE WHOLE PLAN IN ADVANCE.

If God had shown me my life today back when I was young and starting out, I would have run from my calling, or worse, I would have tried to manipulate and "help" God make things happen. I may have become arrogant. I may have thought I was all that and

* Joel Osteen (Joel Osteen Ministries), Facebook, August 6, 2019, www.facebook.com/101306095226/posts/if-god-showed-you-what-he-has-in-store-where-hes-taking-you-it-would-not-only-ex/10162392173295227/.

a bag of chips. I may have gotten too big for my britches, and I'm 100 percent sure I would have jacked everything up.

The person I was *then* could not have handled the reality of my life *now*. And so God didn't show me. He knew I needed to schlep it out day by day, obedient to the next right thing, and the next right thing after that, so that I wouldn't think too lowly or too highly of myself at any given time.

Listen, if God hasn't given you the whole picture yet, count your blessings. Most of us can't handle the whole picture. It's better to see only the next step, and not everything that's coming our way. This allows you room to grow and room to evolve without the pressure of an end result or an end date.

Don't stress that you don't know where you are headed. You know the One who is setting your course. Do you trust His navigation system? That's all that matters.

If you're stuck, stop looking ahead, and focus on the next step. And then the step after that, and then the step after that. It's not as hard. You just need twenty seconds of insane courage most of the time to start that Facebook page. To set up that coffee meeting. To list something for sale on your website.

If you are stuck, scared, or overwhelmed, is there something right there in front of you that you can't get away from? That may be your key to freedom?

It only takes twenty seconds of insane courage to hit the go button. Or make the call or start the conversation. And you can do anything for twenty seconds!

You can get unstuck. You can take the first step to the rest of your life.

And you can do it without knowing where it's going or why you're doing it.

Because fear is NOT the boss of you.

(And by the way, the start is so much better than the middle.

The middle is what separates the ladies from the girls, when the sexy excitement has worn off and now you've just gotta do the work. The messy middle is where all the frustration pops up. It's mundane. It's drudgery. It feels like swimming upstream against a current. So trust me when I say, enjoy the scary start.)

YOU CAN TAKE *the next* STEP WITHOUT KNOWING WHERE YOU'RE GOING OR WHY YOU'RE *doing it.*

If you find the courage to start, God will work in mysterious ways to bring you exactly to the place where He wants you to be. You know what I mean? When it comes to God, it's never about what we think it's about. I have no idea how He can string together seemingly unrelated things, but He does.

He positions you in a job so you meet that guy you end up marrying.

He positions you in a neighborhood so you can begin to have conversations with a neighbor who will wind up being a business partner.

He gets me interested in hip-hop dancing, because . . . well, I don't know yet. I just know that it probably has nothing to do with dancing. I'm sure the hip-hop dance class will be the gateway drug to something else He has for me, just like He used the painting business as a gateway drug to introduce me to clients who wanted me to pray for them.

For all I know, hip-hop dance class could be the thing that causes me to run for public office. LOL.

All I can do is wait and see. And trust. Because God is faithful, and His plans are always so much bigger than mine—a truth I think about every time I look at our house.

About five years ago, I began wanting a new home. We'd been in our old home for about a decade longer than I thought we would be, and we had three growing kids, and okay, I always have the itch for a new home. I love houses. I love decorating. I love putting together an environment that feels good and right to my family and friends.

The trouble was, I also had champagne taste on a Budweiser budget.

Jason and I put our old house on the market and expected it to sell quickly. It wasn't huge, but I'd been blogging pictures of it for more than a decade. It was all over Pinterest, all over Facebook. Our house had been photographed for magazines, TV stations had done segments on it, and we'd had countless requests to put it on tours.

I was arrogant enough to think that people would be able to see past our things and past our very specific taste to imagine our house as their own. Boy, was I wrong. The report back from the realtors was we needed to depersonalize it. Ouch.

To make it worse, I had found a new house I wanted to buy. I had even gone to the house and walked around it seven times (like the story of the walls of Jericho in the Bible), which probably freaked out the neighbors. I also anointed the corners of the property with salad dressing that I had in my truck from Olive Garden (hey, God can work with anything!). I believed that house was ours. But our current home *would not sell*.

It took six weeks to get our first offer, and then that fell through. The second offer came in, and the buyers changed their minds overnight. The third offer came, but we could not agree on a price. And by then, the house we wanted had sold.

We decided to stay put, to remodel and update a little more. In between my hissy fits, I tried to be content and hopeful that we would upgrade homes sooner rather than later.

Then I started having dreams. Dreams of living by water. Dreams of standing by water. Dreams of houses near water. Water, water, water. I started making notes in my phone about my dreams because they were so unbelievably vivid that I just knew that God was trying to tell me something. I didn't know what, but I was encouraged.

Four years later. In the summer of 2018, a different house that we liked came up for sale. This time, everything seemed to be working in our favor, because within days, we had an offer on our house that we accepted.

So we put an offer in on the home we wanted to buy, but so did someone else. The same day. What on earth, Lord? We ended up in a bidding war, and after days of duking it out and waiting, we lost the house to a cash buyer. (Side note: That will never happen to us again. I told my husband that day that next time we will have enough money to buy our dream house in cash. #goals.)

Now, we had three kids, a goldendoodle, a business, and thirty days to figure out where to live. Our house was sold and the one we wanted was gone. Trust me when I tell you we looked at everything in our price range. We weren't being ultra picky. But it was January, and the market was not hopping.

Our realtor, feeling our desperation, put out feelers about houses that could potentially be coming on the market. That's how we heard about a home that my painting company had done some work in ten years ago. It was *way* outside our budget, like 50 percent higher than our budget, but I wanted "to just go see" anyway.

Famous last words, right?

When we got there, we found out the homeowners were in no hurry to go anywhere and weren't even certain they wanted to move. So, not the best-case scenario. And did I mention that it was way outside our budget?

But Jason and I had the strangest feeling this was our home. It backs up to a gorgeous pond, and off the pond is a creek. Plus, there's a beautiful pool complete with fountains and waterfalls. It is a house surrounded by water, just like in my dreams.

And so we made the owners an offer.

We weren't sure how we would make the mortgage, but I knew God was gonna take care of it. He would protect us from what wasn't ours and give us what was.

And did He ever.

We got the house. And two weeks after we bought the home, the revenue from my coaching business multiplied four times over, to seven figures. I couldn't believe it.

That's just like God, though. Once you get on board with what He wants, He will make a way.

The first house we wanted four years before, the salad-dressing house, was not God's plan for us. Losing it hurt like you-know-what at the time, but if we had bought *that*, we would have missed *this*.

The second house, the one we got outbid on, wasn't God's best for us either.

I would have *never* dreamed this house was the one for us, my friend. It was so much more than we could have ever imagined it would be. But God knew.

How is this our life? I don't know, but I do know that God's vision for my future is always so much bigger than mine. I've learned not to ask God for what I think I want, but only to prepare me for what He is about to give me. Make me into who I need to be to handle what You have for me. Don't give me and my family more than what we are ready for.

Now, I'm not saying that if you follow God, He will give you a nice big house. Just read the story of Joseph or the book of Job and you'll know that some believers are called to unbelievable suffering.

But if you're in a season of suffering, believe God has a plan for you and somehow, somewhere in the future, He will work it all out for your good.

If you have an idea that you can't get away from, get ready. It very well could be God. And if you feel like you're supposed to be doing something, even if it doesn't make sense, and you have no idea what it will lead to . . . that's probably God too. Don't try to figure it out; just take the first step. Remember, friend, if you said yes to God, you said yes to *His* plan. That might look like a hip-hop dance class or waiting four years for the home He has planned for you. But you will never know until you take the first step.

Lord, MAKE ME INTO WHO I NEED TO BE TO HANDLE WHAT *You have* FOR ME.

So what step can you take TODAY? One step. Today. What will it be?

Can you do it right now? I double-dog dare you.

And in the next chapter, I'm gonna tell you what is likely to happen NEXT. Brace yourself.

part

FIVE

WHAT HAPPENS NEXT?

THE BIGGER THE *call* ON YOUR LIFE, THE MORE *resistance* YOU'LL GET.

chapter seventeen

WHEN IT ALL GOES TO HECK IN A HANDBASKET

> *Most of us have two lives. The life we*
> *live, and the unlived life within us.*
> *Between the two stands Resistance.*
> —STEVEN PRESSFIELD,
> *THE WAR OF ART*

I wish I could tell you that once you start to get unstuck and move in the direction of the things you are called to do despite your fear, the tough work will be over and it will be all rainbows and unicorns and lucky charms from here on out. But nothing could be further from the truth.

We've talked before about how there is an enemy of your soul who wants you to stay stuck. He wants you to stay broke and broken. And he is going to throw a hissy fit when you begin to get unstuck and do what God is asking you to do to change your life.

The bolder you become, the more you begin to walk toward freedom, the more you press toward what God has for you on this side of heaven, the more pushback you are probably going to get. This is resistance.

Resistance means "the attempt to prevent something by action or argument." In other words, resistance is when things get hard because it feels like everything is going against you.

Here are some things I believe:

The more stuck you used to be, the more resistance you'll face.
The bigger the call on your life, the more resistance you'll get.
The greater the impact you are about to have on people, the more resistance you may get.

And I'm sorry about all that.

But if you are an absolute mess or you are stucker than stuck, you should be encouraged. These are great signs. Painful ones, but great, nonetheless.

Saved in the notes on my phone is a quote from my pastor, Jonathan O'Reilly: "It's not supposed to be easy. 'Easy' never changed the world."

Not that my desire has ever been to change the world. In the beginning of getting unstuck and creating a life outside of average, I just wanted to change our checkbook. Then I wanted to change our family. And now I want to change *your* life.

And let me tell you, there's been plenty of resistance in all that.

I knew writing this book would bring on some resistance, but Lord have mercy, did I have to fight to get this thing done. I've told you already about how I started three times, changing focus and tossing out tens of thousands of words.

When I finally started the draft of the book you're now holding, it was summer break and there were four kids home all the time. Then someone decided we needed another puppy this summer (#guilty), and with all the things, it was too hard to focus at home. But the clock was ticking.

So Jason decided to check me into a hotel to finish the last few chapters of the book.

First, I went to the wrong hotel. That caused confusion, which is never from God.

Then I bumped another vehicle in the parking lot while I was parking. (Sorry, honey. I didn't think I was that close.) That caused panic, which is never from God.

I got to my room, and the iPad I was using to write the book was dead. (Seriously?)

Then I got a phone call from a dear friend who just received a cancer diagnosis (I was heartbroken).

Then one of my team members quit. (Worst timing ever.)

Then a well-meaning family member texted, saying she couldn't believe I would leave home for two nights, "because won't the kids miss you?" (Oh geez. Guilt is always great, isn't it?)

It was one thing after another for the first few hours. I couldn't think clearly, let alone put words on a page. And I absolutely believe that every single one of these things was a distraction to deter me from the big work that was at hand.

Any time you find yourself in the middle of "one thing after another," you have resistance. Any time you ask, "What else can possibly go wrong?" you are experiencing resistance.

None of us are immune to things going sideways as soon as we try to get unstuck. And none of us are immune to the resistance of distraction either. Oh, distraction . . . it's such a sneaky one.

As the old saying goes, "If the enemy cannot *discourage* you, he will do his best to *distract* you." And isn't that so true?

Your car breaks down right after you put a deposit on that new event location. That's a distraction.

Your kid breaks an arm the weekend of your first business conference. That's a distraction.

You get a call that one of your children has head lice, and someone needs to pick them up from school right away just as you're getting ready to take the stage at your biggest event. That's a distraction. (#truestory. Mr. Magic took our little one to a lice removal place—thank You, Lord, for people who will even do such a thing—only to find out our little one did *not* have head lice. Meanwhile, I was across the country at a huge event and trying *not* to think about how my own head was itching. What a distraction!)

The enemy of your soul will distract your mind to keep you from doing what you should do. It's pathetic how much he does it and how often we fall for it.

When crap begins to hit the fan as you step out in courage and faith, you cannot be surprised. Please.

No one, and I mean no one, is exempt from the resistance of distraction.

But distraction isn't the only kind of resistance that may try to stop you when you start doing what you're called to do.

Resistance can look like pushback. The city won't approve your permit. Your application is rejected.

Resistance can come from the people who are closest to you, which we talked about a lot in chapter 5. People say dumb things. They don't build you up. They may not even know that what they're saying or what they're doing is messing with your mind, but it does. And it's hard when it comes from people you love, sometimes even the people you live with. Oh, the stories I've heard.

Resistance also looks like procrastination.

I'm most vulnerable to the resistance of procrastination when I feel super vulnerable about what I'm doing. This book feels big. The writing feels important. Especially as we get close to the end, it's way easier to look at Facebook than it is to dig deep. It's much easier for me to rearrange photos on my phone than it is to get vulnerable on the page. It will make things harder on me later, because my deadline and God's timeline aren't changing, but in the moment, procrastination feels so good.

Procrastination is a form of resistance that jams us up. Makes us late. Piles one thing after another on top of another. And all because we choose to feel good now rather than do the uncomfortable thing now that will benefit us later.

Procrastination is to your future like a shopping spree on a credit card is to your finances. It's easy to let it slide in the moment, but down the road you'll kick yourself in the butt for it.

Procrastination and greatness cannot go hand in hand. "Procrastination is the arrogant assumption that God owes you another chance to do tomorrow what He gave you the chance to do today," says Bishop Rosie O'Neal. You may need to read that twice. Ouch!

Procrastination AND GREATNESS CANNOT GO HAND IN HAND.

Procrastination is a mask that we wear to cover our fear. We convince ourselves that we'll just hold off until we're "ready." We decide to wait until we can put out something that's perfect. But ready is a lie, and perfect is impossible. No one is ever ready. But often we procrastinate in hopes that at a later time, we will feel more equipped. Remember what we talked about before, though? Confidence and feeling ready come from experience. We don't need to be ready. We just need to be willing.

That first step doesn't need to be perfect. There's a flip side to procrastination that will trip us up as well, and that's perfectionism.

Perfectionism means you are doing it all, all the time, and it's all gotta be just right.

Perfectionism is the kissing cousin to pride, and is its own form of resistance. Perfectionism says, "I am more concerned with self-preservation than I am with putting out to the world something that's good enough."

But that's a lie. Perfectionism is an excuse that people use to cover up fear.

Perfectionists are just as scared as the rest of us, but somehow the idea of waiting until it's perfect *sounds* honorable.

Trust me when I say perfectionism is a form of resistance and it is keeping you little. It's keeping you stuck. It's keeping you in bondage.

I heard a podcast once where a woman talked about how we need to feel comfortable putting B-work out into the world. I agree!

That piece of furniture you are painting doesn't have to be perfect to put it up for sale. Put it up when it's good enough and learn from the experience to make the next one better.

This book manuscript doesn't have to be perfect before I turn it in (I'm talking to myself right now). It just has to be good enough.

Your cupcake-decorating skills don't have to be perfect before you take your first order; they're good enough now to make your customers happy. And with experience, you'll get better.

Friend, if you are waiting for it to be perfect, you're making an excuse and you are putting off until tomorrow what could be good enough today.

Please don't partner with procrastination.

Another form of resistance is rehashing in our mind all the ways we have messed up in the past. We want to do this if things start to all go sideways.

We flip through those mental Rolodexes (are you old enough to remember those?), rehashing all we did wrong or failed at in the past.

That last time you tried to start a business. Look how that ended up.

The other time you started a relationship, and it ended so badly.

Perhaps you remind yourself of those twenty pounds you keep losing and regaining. Losing and regaining. (Guilty.)

Those doubts that we talked about back in chapter 7, the ones that were holding you back in the first place, won't let go just because you've set out to do what God calls you to do.

Resistance will throw you off your game if you let it. So don't let it. Realize what it is, and then keep on keepin' on.

And know the more the resistance, the bigger the prize, or something like that, right? Hopefully. But even if the prize isn't bigger, you've done your job . . . you've been obedient.

The enemy wants to discourage you. He knows that when a woman acts, and sticks with it and does what she knows she should, she is a force to be reckoned with. He knows the potential you have, not because he knows everything like God does, but he knows enough to know that every chosen child of God has an influence on this side of heaven. So friend, if you have read this book up till now, and you've started to really hear God and recognize His calling in your life, and you're ready to step out in obedience to that calling and act with courage . . . I want you to anticipate resistance. Don't be shocked when life seems to push back. Instead, say, "Oh yes, Jennifer said there would be days like this."

Resistance will come when you start something new. It will haunt you through the messy middle. And it will ramp up whenever you're about to level up. I've seen so many women go through a season when they feel like the wheels are falling off, and it's always right before the promotion, or the spiritual breakthrough, or whatever it is for them. The enemy is putting in overtime to get people to give up when their breakthrough is right around the corner. They just cannot see it.

I heard a sermon once that talked about rockets in outer space.

I'm no astronaut, but I have seen Ben Affleck in *Armageddon* a handful of times, so I feel like I know a thing or two about rockets. LOL.

And I know that they shake insanely right before they break through the sound barrier, or the next galaxy, or whatever it is they break through. The point isn't where they are going. The point is, if you were on that ship, you would think the entire rocket was about to explode. Everything is shaking and jumping and looking like it's about to fall apart . . . and then there's silence. Peace. They have broken through.

RESISTANCE *will ramp* UP WHENEVER YOU'RE ABOUT TO LEVEL UP. THE DEVIL DOESN'T OPPOSE THINGS THAT DON'T *matter*.

This is how resistance looks to you when you're about to level up. God may be prompting you to keep going, but it's gonna feel like all hell is breaking loose. Can you hold on another little bit?

The bigger your battle, the bigger the victory. The bigger the test, the bigger the testimony. The tougher the lesson, the bigger the blessing.

It's gonna be hard. It's supposed to be. If it weren't hard, everyone would be doing it. And the devil doesn't oppose things that don't matter. What you are doing *matters*. It counts toward eternity.

I know you're bumping up against a lot of "stuff." But are you willing to go to battle for what you want for you and your family? Will you fast and pray for your future? Will you do it scared? Will you ignore what others think and say because you know that God's call on your life matters more than their pettiness? Will you be obedient even when it isn't convenient? When you are up to your neck in resistance?

Doing what God asks you to do, living in your purpose, and walking in your calling *will* be hard. Being obedient will be hard.

But also watching your purpose pass you by because you were too scared to step into it . . . that will be hard also.

Regret is hard. It's all hard. It's supposed to be.

So pick your hard.

I pray you pick wisely. I'm rooting for you.

chapter eighteen

THE MAGIC IS IN
THE DOING

*How long will you put off what
you are capable of doing to continue
what you are comfortable doing?*
—JAMES CLEAR

The good news is that you made it through a book that basically tells you to do the things you are scared to do.

You've worked through seventeen chapters that call you out on the carpet and call you up to something higher. And you're still here. You are my people.

I have to tell you that as I was writing this book, God was making me live this all out in real time.

I want nothing more than to see women living fully in their purpose, to see them living fully in freedom, and to see them doing the big, hard, and scary things that are put in front of them on this side of heaven. And I feel almost desperate to do my part in raising up a group of women who are not just talking the talk but who are actually walking the walk.

I want to see women who are not just hearers of the Word but actual doers of the Word too (James 1:22).

But this isn't the book I thought I was going to write.

God made me restart this book four times, because I wasn't doing what He said. (Insert crying laughing emojis, 'cuz it was all my fault.) He knew I couldn't write a precious book that was just going to tickle your ears (2 Timothy 4:3) and sell well. Those are a dime a dozen.

No, I know I will get to heaven and be responsible for how I led people in this book either closer to Christ or closer to themselves. And that's not a chance I'm willing to take.

I had to write something that is going to provoke you to *action*. I had to do my best to convince you that God has a plan for your life, it's a good one, it's gonna require you to do some hard things, and then let's get on with it.

So many women out there are just living their lives by the seat of their pants. They have no real plan for what they want to get out of this one lifetime. They don't understand the eternal ramifications of the decisions they are making. They don't realize how their indecision *is* a decision and will affect their children and their children's children. I can't bear to watch you be one of them.

They don't understand that they don't need confidence; they need courage. They're merely surviving each day until they eventually die with a list full of regrets and what-ifs and if-onlys. And that breaks my heart.

There is more to life than that, sis. You were made for more.

Before we land this plane, we need to establish and agree that it is okay to want more or different or better for your life. And it's okay to want something different or better, even if you aren't certain of what those things are.

Wanting more does not mean that you are unsatisfied with where you are. It doesn't mean you aren't content, especially you ladies who come from religious backgrounds. You can want more and still be content.

Wanting more does not equal dissatisfaction. Wanting more just means wanting more.

We can adore our firstborn child and still want another kiddo.

We can love our body at its current size and still aspire to change how we look in a swimsuit.

We can have a wonderful biz and still want to take it to the next level.

We can be giving at church but still want to give more.

Wanting more does *not* have to come from a place of greed or a position of jealousy or discontent. I think we were made to want more. This is why I gave my life to Christ. I sensed there was more available to me. And there is more available to you too.

You've read an entire book that tells you if you want more, you have to get yourself unstuck and start *doing* something, even if you're afraid.

Doing is what helped me leave home at seventeen, buy a home at twenty-one, take an online business from nothing to $3 million a year in just a few years. *Doing* is what allowed us to buy the home of our dreams and take in a four-year-old at the ripe old age of forty-seven.

Dreaming is great, but the *doing* is what matters.

Do what you're scared to do. Do what needs to be done. Do what God says. Do because your kids need to see it. Do because your future depends on it.

I'm not telling you to get unstuck because you need to earn God's love or because you aren't good enough where you are. And I'm not telling you to be busy all the time, because goodness, girl, we gotta rest.

I'm telling you to do something because I believe you have

incredible gifts and talents and ideas, yet you continue to stay small because of fear. And that ain't okay.

Ladies, *it is time.*

Get up and get going. You have one life, one chance to do what needs to be done.

You don't have time to waste or whine or put off or give excuses. Tomorrow is not even guaranteed.

There is no time to procrastinate or stall any longer.

He calls us each to *something.* And 99 percent of you reading this right now already know what something God is calling you to do.

It may be applying for a job, or moving across town, or starting a book club, or reaching out to someone for a collaboration. It may be to get your adoption paperwork finished, start a grief group, or get your butt back to a gym.

Whatever you sense God asking you to do, or whatever dream you have in your heart that you want to attempt, it will require that you get off the sofa, get off Pinterest, and start doing something about it to the glory of God.

Yes, there is a time for reflection, and a time for prayer, and a time for journaling and setting your intentions. But at some point, it's time to get up and start.

Many a woman has died with a journal full of goals and intentions and dreams, with none of them realized on this side of heaven.

You cannot continue to pray and pray and pray, asking God to make a way when you refuse to take a step.

You cannot ask God to show you what He wants you to do if you've been ignoring what He's been whispering in your ear for years.

You can't expect God to give you the full picture, the whole enchilada, when you won't even do the *next thing* He's asking you to do.

When everything is said and done, we want God to say when we arrive in heaven, "Well *done*, good and faithful servant." He won't say, "Well *thought*, good and faithful servant" or, "Well *planned*, good and faithful servant" or even, "Well *prayed*, good and faithful servant."

There is only one praise the Bible says He will give you: "Well *done*, good and faithful servant."

So what do you need to do today?

Scrap the goal setting. Do something.

Scrap the intentions. Do something.

Scrap the meditation. Do something.

Scrap the journaling. Do something.

Scrap everything, because it's time to stop thinking and start doing.

Whatever it is, start.

Even if it's wrong, start.

You've seen in these chapters how God works with people in motion. He can fix it if it's wrong. God has the full ability to reroute you, to pull you back, to bypass your plans and switch your directions once you start. But as the saying goes, God cannot steer a parked car. He can't do anything with inaction.

My friend, I've told you a lot of stories about myself in this book, and most of them don't make me look too good. I promise you that I am not smart enough on my own to run a business or write a book. I was not talented enough to get famous for my painting.

But what I am is obedient. I say yes. Now, I may go kicking and screaming, but the cry of my heart will always be, "Here I am, Lord, pick me."

He wants to pick *you* too. The Bible says He is looking for a girl who is willing to say yes (well, that's not exactly it, but . . .).

Are you ready to say yes? Are you ready to do it today?

Because we already established chapters ago that delayed obedience is disobedience. Making no decision is a decision.

Don't let the start stop you.

Yes, you'll look like a beginner.

Yes, you may be the youngest in that group or the oldest in that class.

Yes, you may sweat through your shirt and shake in your shoes.

But you will still be doing what you're called to do.

If that thought isn't stirring your soul, then perhaps you are not desperate enough yet. Perhaps you don't want it bad enough yet. Perhaps God hasn't convinced you of your purpose enough yet. Perhaps you don't feel the pressure of time and have not realized yet that this lifetime goes by so stinking fast.

But you will. And this book will be here for you then too.

There is more to life, my friend, than endless diapers, soul-sucking jobs, barely scraping by, and white-knuckling through your days.

This is not God's best life for you. He came so that you would have *life* and have it to *abundance* (John 10:10). Not so you would have lack. Not so you would live in fear. Not so you would be confused. Not so you would stay stuck.

> YOU CANNOT ASK GOD TO SHOW YOU WHAT HE WANTS YOU TO DO IF YOU'VE *been ignoring* WHAT HE'S BEEN WHISPERING IN YOUR EAR *for years.*

He paid a price so that you could live wildly and boldly and freely.

He created you to be a free woman. Not stuck and scared and overwhelmed. And you have both the capability and responsibility to change your mind and think differently.

And if a woman changes her mind, she can change her life.

But the kind of life you long for doesn't come by playing small. That life doesn't come from the couch. It comes from getting in the game. It comes from deciding to *do* something today that will take you one step closer to the life you want. It comes from leaning in to what God is trying to whisper in your ear. And then having the courage to walk it out. Regardless of your feelings. Regardless of your qualifications.

And that, my friend, is a life worth living.

Fear is not the boss of you, and THAT is worth celebrating. I'm rooting for you.

XOXO, Jen

STILL STUCK?
THIS IS NOT YOUR
MOMMA'S THERAPY

For some of you, reading these stories and hearing me say it's time to act is all you need. For others, though, the pull of the couch is still strong. You have read every line of what's here and know that it is truth, but you cannot get yourself unstuck.

I get it. Sometimes what we need isn't a book, but a one-on-one kick in the pants. I've gone through periods like this when I needed someone else to step in and walk me through my own unsticking, because I could not get out of my own head.

There is a woman in our church, and she does counseling. Now, this is not your momma's counseling. This is Holy Spirit-led counseling designed to let God lead you through your healing. It's called "inner healing ministry" and it's p-o-w-e-r-f-u-l.

This type of counseling isn't about scheduling weekly meetings to talk about the same issues every week. No, these sessions are all about forgiveness, repentance, rejecting lies, and replacing them with God's truths . . . in a nanosecond.

I started going to see this counselor about five years ago,

because I just couldn't get over the hump of being worried about what people thought of me. This was something I knew had held me back for years, and when I was sick enough of my stuckness, I knew it was time to call in someone else.

A typical session in the counselor's office starts with prayer (#obviously). Then she asks what I want to talk about. I say, "I am worried about this person or this situation or this whatever," and then she says, "Okay, so let's ask God what He says about that."

That's it. No lying back on couches and talking forever about feelings. She goes straight to the source. And when you ask God what He thinks, you'd best hold on to your britches. God has a lot to say if you just ask and listen. And when you are having a counseling session with *Him*, administered through a woman like her, breakthrough and healing are just one question and one answer away.

So the first time I went, we prayed and repented through the stronghold of me caring more about what others thought than I did about what God wanted, and I was good for a hot minute.

But then a few months later, other things popped up, because overcoming fear isn't a one-time thing. God is continually working things out in us and through us.

And so over the last few years, I have gone to this counselor seeking God for freedom from all these things that were keeping me stuck:

- I needed to forgive myself for dumb things I'd done.
- I had forgiven my husband for things, but I needed help to forget them.
- I was stressed because the business was growing fast, and imposter syndrome was rearing its ugly head.
- I was wondering if God was going to pull the rug out from under us, and we would lose it all.
- I was putting incredible pressure on myself to keep all the plates spinning, as if it was all up to me.

- Jason and I had to pray together with the counselor to get rid of some of the generational junk that was on our family.
- Many times I needed to talk about not wanting to hurt someone's feelings, not wanting to offend anyone, and wanting to keep everyone—including strangers—happy, and how such people-pleasing behavior was affecting me.

I share that list of "junk" with you so that you understand that your own junk is normal. We all have our stuff to work through . . . every single one of us. So if you've been reading this book and feeling convicted, but something's still holding you back, it may be time to work through your issues with a professional. There is no shame in that. Smart people get help when they can't do things on their own.

Yes, it may cost money. Most good things do. But there comes a point when your mental and emotional and spiritual freedom are worth the cost.

This is heart and soul work that you will never regret.

Not sure where to start? Try this:

- Call your church office.
- Google Christian counselors in your area.
- Find someone who specializes in "Going to the Core" ministry like Lorrie does.
- Look for programs like Oaks of Righteousness Ministry, Discover Freedom Ministries, or Plumbline Ministries, which are all programs designed to drill down to what has been said or done to you to make you believe lies about yourself, and how to break the lies so you can live the free life God has for you.

Good luck, sis. Holy Spirit-led therapy has saved my marriage and my business. It may save yours too.

appendix two

I SAVED THE BEST PART FOR LAST

The Lord announces the word,
and the women who proclaim
it are a mighty throng.
—PSALM 68:11

Hey, you. Congratulations, you made it to the back of the book, where the good stuff is.

I know you may have landed here simply because you are a rule follower and read every word on every page. But you also may have landed here because you're not sure about some of the stuff I've been talking about on these pages. What's with all this religion stuff? The more I talked, the less you were sure that you know the same God that I know.

Maybe you gave your life to Christ once but have since walked away. It's okay, sis. You can come back. I did.

When I was getting ready to host my first Equipped women's conference, I kept feeling that God wanted me to do an altar call at the end of it—the kind where I ask people to commit to Jesus.

I've told you in this book how that made me wrestle with God. I told Him I didn't know what to say. I'm not a professional pray-er. I teach people how to get more followers on Facebook, for goodness' sake.

But God kept nudging. And the night before the conference, I started to google "how to lead people to the Lord" and "words for a salvation prayer."

And then I remembered, Oh yeah, I don't have to do it perfectly. I just gotta do it. Courage, not confidence, right? I'm taking my own advice here!

And you know what? Knowing nothing about how to lead people to Christ made me the perfect one to lead unsure people to Christ. All through the weekend, I stood onstage and talked about doing things afraid, so it was super fitting that at the very end, God made me stand in front of those women and do something afraid.

I want you to know that I still don't know what to say here, but it doesn't matter. What matters is that you have a God in heaven who adores you. He put you here on this earth for such a time as this. He loved you enough to send His Son to earth to die on a cross for you. It's okay that you don't understand it all. I don't either.

But what I do know is that you are no accident and no afterthought. You are not too big of a hot mess for God to handle.

He is crazy in love with you and wants so badly to see you walk in freedom.

I'll never forget the day I gave my life to the Lord when I was sixteen years old. I didn't understand what I was doing. But I was in a room full of church people who had something I wanted. They seemed to be full of hope and joy, and although I didn't know what it was, it pulled at my heartstrings like the clearance section at Hobby Lobby.

I wanted whatever they had. So when the pastor asked people to come forward if they wanted to give their life to Christ, and my best friend Rachel asked me if I wanted to go up front, there was no way I could say no.

Friend, I would love to invite you to come up front too. And just like Rachel did that day, I'll hold your hand and go on up with you.

There is a hole in your heart that only God can fill. Please trust me on this.

There is no drug, no shopping spree, no raw cookie dough, and no man on this side of heaven that can fill that ache in your soul. Trust me, I tried.

You've been trying to fit a round peg into a square hole for way too long. It's time to try something different, my friend.

Let God take His rightful place in your heart and heal you of all your hurts.

Giving your life to Christ is hands-down the most powerful, wisest, best decision that you will ever make for yourself.

And you don't have to be at a church or at a conference to do it.

Just read this . . . out loud. Or silently. God doesn't care either way.

Dear Lord,
I need You.
I have tried things my way long enough.
I am tired of struggling and feeling empty.
I am tired of doing things my way and living for myself.
I ask for Your forgiveness.
I receive You as my Lord and Savior.
Help me to do things Your way, Lord.
Help me to trust You.
Help me to live my life for You and with You.
In Jesus's name.
Amen.

And that's it, friend. Giving your life to God doesn't have to be fancy. It's not a bunch of rules. It's a relationship that God desires, and I pinkie swear . . . your life will never be the same.

I'm so honored to get to be a part of your journey.

And look, let me give you some advice. I became a Christian in high school and went with my bestie Rachel to church every chance I had after that. But it didn't take long after I left for college to throw God out the window because I wasn't surrounded by Christians anymore.

A coal separated from the fire will quickly go out on its own.

So that's why you need to get into a good Bible-based church near you. If you don't know where to start, well, I go to a nondenominational church. You could just ask God to show you a nondenominational church near you. Or ask Siri. She will help. Or go to Facebook and ask your friends if anyone can recommend a good Bible-based Christian church near you.

You'll have people come out of the woodwork with responses. I promise you.

Then go. Meet people. Plug in. Get a Bible and start reading it. (There are lots of versions, so don't get overwhelmed. Pick the one with language that speaks to you. I prefer the NIV.) And never look back.

I need to say here that if a church has wounded you in the past, I am so, so sorry. Please give church and us knuckleheaded believers another chance. We will never be perfect, but we want to do this life with you.

And finally, friend, I am sooooo stinkin' proud of you. After reading a book about doing hard things, you did the biggest, hardest thing you could have ever done today. Even if we never meet face-to-face in this lifetime, I rejoice knowing that I will meet you in eternity one day.

All of heaven is rejoicing on your behalf. Your life will never be the same. Every hour, every week, every month writing this book was worth it for just one woman to have her life changed.

I am ridiculously proud of you and happy for you.

Thank you for allowing me to be just a tiny piece of your story. The rest of your own book awaits. And I can't wait to see it.

> All my love and in Him,
> *Jennifer*

P.S. If you did give your life to Christ today, I want to know!!!!! Would you email me at jen@jenniferallwood.com? I want to rejoice in the news with you.

ACKNOWLEDGMENTS

First and foremost, thank You, Lord, for saving my soul and for entrusting me with this message. I will never take this platform for granted. I owe it all to You.

Next, I want to honor my husband, Jason. HOW IS THIS EVEN OUR LIFE? We were a couple of knuckleheads, but look what God has done! There is no one else I would want to be on this crazy ride with . . . and honestly, no one else on this side of heaven could handle me. You are my biggest supporter, and you believed I could write this book even on the many days when I did not. You put me up in fancy hotels and took care of all the kids and fed me a perfect balance of green drinks and sea salt chocolates until my deadlines were all met. Thank you for loving me so well. You are stuck with me until my last breath! I love you.

Noah, you are my favorite. Don't tell the other kids. You were the first to make me a mom, and I had no idea my heart was capable of that kind of love. You are a fascinating combination of challenge and compassion, stubborn yet sensitive, confrontational yet adorable. The Lord has anointed you as a prayer warrior, and I thank you for praying over this book, son. I'm ridiculously proud to be your mom and can't wait to see how you're going to light the world on fire. It's absolutely in you to do so. I love you.

Easton, you are my favorite. Don't tell the other kids. Thank you for who you are. You are self-disciplined, self-motivated, self-governed, and it makes my job as your mom very easy. I love that you hold yourself to a high standard, and I pray that you always respect the line in the sand that you draw for yourself. It's God's line for you also. You have been an absolute joy to raise, and I would adore you even if you weren't my son. I am wild about you and love your peacemaking heart. I can't wait to watch your life unfold. I love you.

Ava, you are my favorite. Don't tell the other kids. From the moment I knew you were a girl, I thanked God for the gift of your very life. I prayed and prayed and prayed for you, and God answered my prayer. You are the most beautiful combination of girlie-girl and wild, daring, hanging-from-the-chandelier adventurer. You are sugar and spice, and I adore both. I have a front row seat watching you grow from our baby girl into a big sister and now into a young lady, and you have done so with absolute grace. You are an absolute treasure, Avababy. I will never get over having you as my daughter. I love you.

Ari, you are my favorite. Don't tell the other kids. Today I found out your other mom, your first mom, is going to let me be your forever mom. My heart is rejoicing. I will never take her sacrifice or my job lightly. Oh, how we both love you! In many ways you saved our family, Ari . . . and we didn't even know we needed saving. You are so adored and so loved and so ridiculously resilient. I can't even wrap my head around what God must have in store for your life. I pinkie swear to love and protect you from here until forever. I love you.

Mom, I hope I've made you proud. Thank you for doing big, hard, and scary things in your own life so that I could be brave with my life too. I love you and still want only you when I am sick. (Do we ever outgrow that?)

Dad, thank you for stepping up and doing what most men wouldn't, and thank you for showing me the value of hard, smart work. You set me up to be a successful entrepreneur. I love you.

Ray and Verda Beeson, my grandparents who are long gone from this earthly life but forever in my heart, told me over and over that I could do and be anything I wanted, and I was crazy enough to believe them. I pray that one day I am half the grandparents they were. (Children, please note that this better be a long, long time from now.)

Rachel, my bestie, thank you for taking me to your home church thirty-two years ago so that I could be introduced to Jesus. And thank you for moving clear across the country to save my butt when I was young and dumb and desperately hurting. I will never be able to repay you for that kind of friendship. I will hang out with you in heaven one day because you were brave enough as a teen to ask me to church. "Thank you" will never seem like enough.

Laura, my armor-bearer and the sister I never had, you are the best friend a girl could ask for. You are fiercely loyal and steadfast to the end. You make me want to be a better wife, mom, and friend. I am forever grateful for your prayer covering and anointing. The devil got it wrong when he came to mess with you. Thank you for fighting the good fight alongside me. I thank God for the gift of your friendship.

Carrie, no one can match your encouragement and your cheerleading. You are ridiculously supportive and wicked smart. Your friendship is a gift available to me only because two strangers sat next to one another at a business conference in Chicago years ago. Don't you love how God brings you exactly who you need exactly when you need them? Thank You, Jesus.

Jill, you've taught me more about the Lord than anyone else

on this side of heaven. You knew this book would happen long before I did. Thank you for all you do to spread the good news. I am proud to know you!

To the Schmudes, the Giambalvos, the Kitches, and the Stanleys—we absolutely love doing life with you. Our friend group is the best there is! Here's to many, many more years of raising kids, Sunday pool parties, and traveling together.

Pastor Phillip and Susan O'Reilly, thank you for pastoring Jason and me for more than twenty years. You have both spent countless evenings on our sofa, helping us sort through our crap and bringing us back to center. You are shining examples of resiliency and listening to God even when it's hard. Thank you for shepherding our hearts so well and for giving us an example worthy of following.

Beth Jusino, my editor, you are the bee's knees, the cat's meow, all that and a bag of chips. You didn't wring my neck when I started this manuscript over with six days to spare. You let me cry when I needed to. Thank you.

Carolyn McCready and the entire team at Zondervan, thank you for taking a chance on me and believing in this call to courage for all women. I hope there are more books to come!

Nena Madonia Oshman, my book agent, I would never bet against you, and I am still half terrified of you. That's what makes you so good at what you do. Thank you for being in my corner. I cannot lose with you there.

Brian Dixon, your support and advice for getting this book from idea to print has been invaluable. You "started with your people" (one being me), and I am so, so grateful for your friendship.

Aimee Decker, thank you for making me look good for the front cover photo of this book. You work magic with my face and a camera. Bless you.

The ladies working with me at Team Allwood—Vicki, Jenna,

Nell, Rachel, Mackenzie, and Cindy—you have no idea how grateful I am for your hard work and loyalty. Thank you for partnering with me as we change the lives of women.

My Facebook friends and Instagram followers, it's only because of people like you following people like me that people like me get to do things like write a book. I am forever grateful for your support and for how you have showed up for and shared my message.

And finally, to my coaching clients and all the women that I will coach in years to come: I am rooting ridiculously hard for you. The only thing that stands between many of you and your success and happiness is being afraid and needing to do it anyway. Go, go, go, my friend. The world is your oyster and it needs what you have!

WAIT! ONE MORE THING
BEFORE YOU LEAVE!

Fear is strong, but our God is SO MUCH STRONGER. I want his Word hidden in your heart, but also smack dab in front of your face as frequently as physically possible.

That's why I've taken every last Scripture I reference in *Fear Is Not the Boss of You* and put them on super pretty verse cards just for you to download.

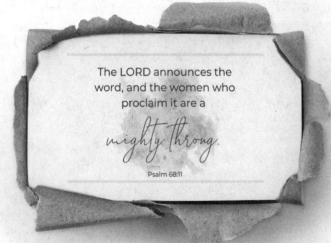

The LORD announces the word, and the women who proclaim it are a *mighty throng*.

Psalm 68:11

Go to www.jenniferallwood.com/gift to print off your free set of Bible verse cards.

Tape them to your mirror, frame them on your desk, make them the background of your phone, heck, put them everywhere you look. The more you read and meditate on these verses, the more you'll be able to rest knowing He's got this and He's got you.